Ruins

Morgan Meis

Published December, 2012
Fallen Bros. Press
6010 South Pacific Coast Highway #9
Redondo Beach CA 90277

ISBN: 978-0615751740

Original Publication:

From **The Smart Set** *(which doesn't preserve dates of publication):*
The Night of the Hunter; Autumn; An Army of Dark Clouds; Winter;
Ruins; The Hudson River; Francis Bacon; Frans Hals; Melville Redux;
Giorgio Morandi; The Pale King; Ostalgia; The Mezzanine.

From **3 Quarks Daily**: A Tribute to European Trains, April 20,
2009; Behind Wire, May 28, 2007; Paterson, New Jersey, September
10, 2007.

From **Virginia Quarterly Review**: Moby Dick (as "The Seaward
Peep: Three writers respond to Moby-Dick"), Summer 2011; Katyn (as
"A Monument to Forgetting"), Fall 2011.

Cover and interior design: © Guillermo Bosch, 2012

For Shuffy

Altered photograph, urban ruin, anonymous (also on cover in color)

CONTENTS..Page

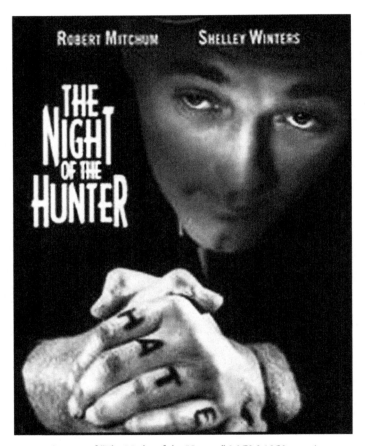

Section of "The Night of the Hunter," MGM 1950s movie poster

The Night of the Hunter

One fine day in the mid 50's, the eminent British actor Charles Laughton and the brilliant, if doomed, American critic James Agee put their minds together with the aim of adapting David Grubb's novel, *The Night of the Hunter*, into a screenplay. Agee was drunk. He couldn't put together a coherent screenplay. But he had the mood right, Southern Gothic, and Laughton slapped that Agee madness together with a noire look and German Expressionist approach. Most of the scenes in the movie are mean and tight. The shadows go on forever. Interiors are framed in pointy triangles of light against the gloom.

Then, of course, there is Robert Mitchum. He plays the preacher with 'hate' tattooed on one set of knuckles and 'love' on the other. He has a particular hatred of women. In prison with a young man who robbed a bank and then hid the money before he was captured, the preacher becomes convinced that the man's two children know where the money is. When he gets out, he goes to find them.

The Night of the Hunter is a nightmare movie. Its leering camera perspective is that of childhood terror. After their mother is killed by the preacher, the children escape on a skiff down the river. That river scene. So strange, so haunting. I don't really have a theory about the shots of animals (a rabbit, a frog, an owl) framed in the foreground as the children drift down the river in the background. Perhaps it is simply what a Mother Goose tale would look like if things went very wrong.

That's what the movie is really about. It's a confirmation of the most essential childhood fear, which is that reality is evil. The children's flight from reality is punctuated by their inability to shake the preacher, who keeps appearing on the horizon riding on a broken down horse and singing the hymn "Leaning on the Everlasting Arms." "Leaning... Leaning..."

It took an outsider, in this case the British Laughton, to tap into the undercurrent in American culture in order to make such a truly disturbing film. Nathaniel Hawthorne is exhumed here, as is Salem, the harsh and millenarian sects and creeds that one could find along the dirt roads of rural America during the First and Second Great Awakenings.

The film was a popular and critical flop when it was released. American popular culture was not particularly in the mood for portrayals of evil in the 1950s. The idea that the devil actually walks amongst us has generally been relegated to those religious gatherings in outdoor tents where everyday folk suddenly speak in tongues.

But darker thoughts are always lurking at the edges of consciousness. As Hannah Arendt used to say, the problem of evil became real, visceral, after the reality of the Second World War. America was protected from some of that in its cultural self-reliance. The genius of *The Night of the Hunter* is to tap into those themes using a purely American idiom.

At the end of the movie, the evil preacher is thwarted by

a goodly woman (played brilliantly by Lillian Gish) and captured by the police. At the trial, the young boy whose mother was murdered cannot bring himself to testify against the preacher. It is an off note in what would otherwise be a happy ending. But the little boy knows something. Evil doesn't go away.

Section of The Corn Harvest, Breugel the Elder, 1565

Autumn

The cool wind coming in from the north, the piles of dead leaves crunching under foot, the sun that hangs lower in the sky with each passing day. It is easy to forget that all these changes used to point to something. The approach of autumn was the transformation in a mode of life, moving us from the work of the last days of the harvest to the hunkering down in preparation for winter.

It is amazing, even now, how quickly the shift in seasons stimulates a transformation of mood. The mind is pulled along by forces lurking in the weather—in the sun and the moon, in the otherwise-unnoticed messages from the grass and the trees. We are changing, they say, and so shall you. You simply can't feel the same on an autumn day as you might feel on one of those bright, intrusive days of early spring. That's what Keats was getting at in his *Ode to Autumn*:

Where are the songs of Spring? Ay, where are they?
Think not of them, thou hast thy music too,—

Spending, as I am, the last days of summer and the

emergent days of autumn in the Flemish parts of Northern Europe, I can't help thinking of the paintings of Peter Breugel the Elder. He didn't paint the seasons as merely aesthetic motifs. He painted them as actors. The seasons make you do things, literally. They make you feel one way and not another, literally. Bruegel managed to paint the compulsion.

It is impossible to stare at Bruegel's autumnal painting, Return of the Herd, for more than a minute or two without becoming autumn-minded in your own head. The dark clouds are creeping this way across the horizon. The animals must be rounded up and brought back over the hills, careless beasts. The barren trees at this crest compel one to pull the coat on a little tighter and cuddle into oneself even if the temperature does not fully warrant it yet. That is what Fall want from us, and the body submits.

I particularly like how the spots of sunshine in the painting act as fragments of memory embedded in the landscape. How quickly summer has faded. But there she is for a moment when the sun hits the still-beiged fields in a glancing blow between cloud formations. Summer still winks a few goodbyes. That is because Fall is a between-season, while Winter and Summer are not. Who knows why? They were just made that way.

We are not, now, dominated by autumn in the way that Bruegel understood it and painted it. There is human achievement in this fact, as well as indefinable loss. Being less at the mercy of the cruel cycles of nature means being more at the mercy of our selves. Shall we call this an ambivalent trade-off? Anyway, it is not hard, even with all the historical changes, to receive the visceral impact of Bruegel's painting. We can still feel the seasonal call, the all-encompassing shift in the mood and way of things that Bruegel gives us with his landscape, a few peasants, and the slowly roaming cows. In that, at least, it is the same autumn as it ever was.

Train, anonymous

A Tribute to European Trains Twenty or Thirty Years Old

My friend was right. You want the older trains, the trains with the compartments enclosing six or eight seats. You want the trains with the sun-washed drapes and the yellow-tinged headrest, marked by decades of not-so-recently-washed hair. You want the train with the sliding glass door that lets you into a narrow hallway along the left side of the train car. You would prefer the train with a rudimentary toilet that flushes by means of a foot pedal, in which, as a man, you can watch yourself pee straight down through the rusty tube onto the track rushing by in a ruffle of wooden slats below. Clickety-clak, clickety-clak. "Do not use the toilet while the train is in or near the station," says the sign.

Europe is a train. The countries are all so close together, train close. A plane is too fast. You must fly over vast quantities of land or sea to get something out of an airplane ride. You have to stare out the window for hours at the unchanging surface of the ocean or the mesmerizing openness, for instance, of the American plains. To understand space in Europe you have to be on a train.

You sit near the window in your compartment. There are the forward-sitters and the backward-sitters. Both have their logic. Forward-sitters like to see what is coming, they tend to feel positive about the European Union. Backward-sitters are a more melancholy lot. They think of Europe as something you grab glimpses of after the fact, after it has already passed us by. Thus we see that space has something to do with time. Thomas Mann said it like this, "All good things take time; so do all great things. In other words, space will have its time. It is a familiar feeling with me that there is a sort of hubris, and a great superficiality, in those who would take away from space or stint it of the time naturally bound up with it." That's an extremely European thought. I'm not sure it's even true, but I like that fact that he said it. Of course, Thomas Mann was Europe. I suppose then, by logical extension, that Thomas Mann was a train.

***

There's a specific way that European women walk. It can't be described but you know it. It is slightly more constrained than an American gait. But it is oddly provocative in being so. You wouldn't use words like shake or shimmy. Maybe you would say, "slink."

Try to slink on a moving train, though. Your ass is getting thrown from one wall to the other. The slink becomes a goddamn catastrophe. It really gets ugly when she gets to those doors between trains. Those doors are the enemy of elegance everywhere. You are a brute when you reach those doors, an animal fighting for survival. This is the realism of trains. Nothing is more extraordinary than an aging European woman with well-tailored slacks sitting alone, by the window, in a compartment, chewing just a bit on the end of her pencil. And nothing is more ridiculous than that same woman stumbling toward the restroom as the train snakes up a pass through the Alps. That is the give and take of a train. The mystery and the baseness.

Do you remember the opening scene of Lars Von Trier's *Zentropa*? The darkness, the camera moving along the train tracks. "You are in Germany," the narrator says. The train, that European train. The narrator counting down from ten. The European train in 1945. What, oh what have you been doing with your trains, Europe? Why is Europe so fucking evil? No one knows. The bread is excellent, though.

Every so often, as the train winds through the European countryside, the tracks will edge up against a local road. You sit staring out the window having given yourself over to the rhythm again, clickety-clack, clickety-clack. Suddenly there is an old man standing at the side of the road, watching the train go by. It all happens quickly, the train is traveling at top speed. But the human eye is fast too. You lock eyes with the old man and it is startling as hell. He is standing still by the road, and you are hurtling past in a compartment. But there is an uncanny intimacy. He is watching you, you are watching him. You both know it. Your eyes have locked. Both of your mouths open just a little, simultaneously. A tiny gasp of mutual shock. The instant is infinite and then gone forever.

***

There is no sadder place than the platform of a train station. I don't know why exactly. I'm reminded of a few lines by John Ashbery.

> *Only the wait in stations is vague and*
> *Dimensionless, like oneself. How do they decide how much*
> *Time to spend in each? One begins to suspect there's no*

Rule or that it's applied haphazardly.
Sadness of the faces of children on the platform,

It is just like that standing on a train platform, vague
and dimensionless. Then Ashbery adds the thought that
it is vague and dimensionless "like oneself." That's a
mean line, ruthless. Why are we so much more exposed
on a train platform than anywhere else? Why does it
expose so accurately our own internal flimsiness? And
that's what you are at a train station, nothing. Standing alone on the concrete platform. Who am I frick-
ing kidding? And it is true that the children are always
looking at you funny. Run away, children, I don't even
exist.

Then the train comes grudgingly to a halt from around
the bend. Trains don't like the station either. Out on
the tracks, flying across the countryside a train is con-
fident and sleek. At the station, it lumbers and shud-
ders to a halt, wasted. Stations break the rhythm of the
experience, upsetting the flow of train-induced reverie.
You feel guilty standing at the station, knowing that
you're the cause of the interruption. But maybe that is
the honesty of the train, too, the stops and starts, the
necessary interruptions. Soon enough you are off again,
sliding across the earth, skirting across the mountains,
rushing along beside the great rivers in their coursing.
This makes the brain slide too, skipping across time,
memories, thoughts that jingle jangle in the evening
light. Yes, my friend was right, you want the older trains,
twenty or thirty years old, and you want to catch that
train just as the light is dying, in an old country where
they don't give a shit about anything anymore because

they know it keeps happening anyway and so they've settled back to enjoy the ride, clickety-clack, clickety-clack, into another nameless night.

Section of "Sunrise with Sea Monsters," J.M.W. Turner, 1845

An Army of Dark Clouds

An army of dark clouds slid over Brooklyn today. They came from the north, whence come the wicked. We don't know who sent them, but we don't have to. Dark forces are dark forces. It was a Romantic painting in Kings County, New York, something, maybe, by J.M.W. Turner.

Charles Baudelaire once said, "Romanticism is precisely situated neither in choice of subject nor exact truth, but in the way of feeling." That's a vague definition perfectly fitting to a vague subject matter. For all the use of words like "precisely" and "exact" it is neither. Romanticism, in short, barely exists. It is more of a mood than a movement. But what is a mood? It's not a mental state exactly. Mood is more like the color of consciousness. But that merely adds vagary to vagary. Fact is, we're still not sure what consciousness is, let alone mood.

On the other hand, life is lived under the umbrella of moods and feelings. The low clouds bring with them low feelings. Space contracts. The kid in the doorway on Atlantic Avenue has his collar pulled up and he's trying to light a cigarette against the wind. The sidewalk is empty but for a ragged cat going nowhere. The clouds keep coming in rows and layers. Armies of darkness.

I am talking, here, about the weather. That most banal of conversation topics. The weather is superficiality at its essence. Except that the weather matters. It is the fundamental tool by which nature adds flavor, color, mood to the variety of our daily experience. Nature is mechanistic in its functioning, tied to the laws of physics that give it rules. But it speaks to us in feelings. The light of a day is "like this." The shadows of winter make the world one way: brittle maybe, precise. The angle of the sun makes the world of summer another way entirely: smeared across the afternoon, vibrating.

That's why so many Romantic artists like the weather. They know that the weather does not make the world, but it does make the world "what it's like." So, the Romantics enjoy writing about the weather, and they enjoy painting the weather. They are cloud watchers and rain walkers. They wait for the light to be just so.

Take "Sunrise with Sea Monsters" by J.M.W. Turner. Painted in 1845, it looks like it could be a work of 20th century Expressionism. The main difference being that Expressionists aimed to express something inner, something subjective. Romantics like Turner look at things the other way round. They show us nature as a force that determines feelings in us. They show us nature as a communicative beast, framing our experience at every moment. The weather makes us, we do not make the weather.

What of the sea monsters, then? Well, for the Romantics, the voice of nature is neither gentle nor benign. It isn't specifically malevolent either. The story is bigger, even more overwhelming in its implications. The weather that nature sends us frames our experience, gives us a set of feelings in which to live. But that frame is sent to us from beyond the limits of experience. It is sent to us from the unknown.

Sunrise in particular is a time of revelation. The world opens up. It is the most fundamental of thresholds, the threshold between night and day, dark and light. And that is a perfect place for monsters to go a lurking. Monsters are a half step between form and formlessness. Their monstrousness comes from their violation of the normal rules of shape and form and function. Monsters are a peak into the beyond, a glimpse behind the veil. And there they are in Turner's painting. The monsters at the edge of day. Are they even there at all? In a moment more they won't be.

I glimpsed them in the clouds today above Brooklyn. Sea monsters in the cracks of light between the long rows of marching clouds. The monsters were murmuring something about the fearsome incomprehensible largeness of the world. They were telling old stories to the Romantics on the Brooklyn streets below.

Barbed Wire, anonymous

Behind Wire

Sometime during the early part of the twentieth century the foundations were laid for a new civilization. Czeslaw Milosz once called it a civilization 'behind wire'. That phrase has stuck with me. That it was a new civilization, a new way of looking at man, there is no doubt. Just what that means for us, now and forevermore, is something we're still thinking about—as we should be. It will take a long time to stew this one over and there is good reason not to rush, not to miss any of the details.

The new civilization behind wire was based on a seemingly contradictory pair of assumptions. One, that human beings are dangerous. Two, that human beings are nothing. But in the end there was a master logic that held these two propositions together. The civilization behind wire was to take dangerous human beings and prove to them, in the brutal schoolyard of experience, that they are, in fact, nothing at all. Dangerous human beings, in the face of their nothingness, tend to become less dangerous. Most of the pupils died convinced. Those that staggered out of the camps alive (sort of) were a mixed and mixed-up bag. Most of them came out simply broken.

Another way to look at it is to see men like Stalin and Hitler as theological figures. They were interested in the soul. They were interested in experimenting with the soul. And with a remarkable audacity that can almost be admired, if with a shudder, they wanted to defeat the human soul. Aleksander Wat, the Polish poet and philosopher who spent some time in the Gulag system, once opined in his extraordinary memoir My Century:

> I want to stress this point: the essence of Stalinism is the re-forging of souls. ... The point was not to correct the five or fifteen million in [the corrective camps] because they were a minority and Stalin was concerned with large numbers, large percentages; the only point was the population as a whole. ... The point was for everyone to feel that threat at every moment, to know that the camps were terrible and that this could not be spoken of because this was something holy, sacral.

The wager at the foundation of the civilization behind wire was a brash one, it was absolute. The bet was that human beings could be made into slaves completely and utterly. The bet was that there is nothing in human 'nature' that makes them any more creatures of freedom than creatures of absolute servility. The bet was that men will become slaves and like it; will, in some cases, thrive in it.

It is unclear exactly what is the final outcome, the final lesson of the civilization behind wire. Did it succeed in its basic proposition and fail for other reasons? How much did it reveal man to be a nothing? How much did it shatter the last illusions of men? These are uncomfortable thoughts, unsettling areas for human inquiry.

That's why the region of literature that deals with the civilization behind wire sits in a special and ghettoized region of the mind. I'll confess a physical feeling of apprehension mixed with something close to electricity when I pick up certain books by Primo Levi, Aleksander Wat, Imre Kertész, Tadeusz Borowski, Danilo Kis, Gustav Herling, Aleksandr Solzhenitsyn, and so on. I'm always sickly amused that such books are often betrayed already on their back covers by the promotional quotes that invariably adorn them. It is as if we are so zealous to inoculate ourselves from these books, to mute their terribleness, that we coat them even on their front and back covers with what amounts to a tissue of protective misrepresentations, lies. We understand that this literature is important, but at the same time we want it to go away.

My copy of Gustav Herling's 'A World Apart: The Journal of a Gulag Survivor' is furnished with a quote from The Observer that opines it "will be read for its humanity and beauty of expression." I suppose that is true. But it would not have been my first choice in characterizing a book that contains the following description of the logic of the civilization behind wire:

"A prisoner is considered to have been sufficiently prepared for the final achievement of the signature only when his personality has been thoroughly dismantled into its component parts. Gaps appear in the logical association of ideas; thoughts and emotions become loosened in their original positions and rattle against each other like the parts of a broken down machine; the driving belts connecting the past with the present slip off their wheels and fall sloppily to the bottom of the mind; all the weights and levers of mind and willpower become jammed and refuse to function; the indicators of the pressure gauges jump as if possessed from zero to maximum and back again. ... the next morning he wakes feeling empty as a nut without a kernel and weak after the inhuman strain to which his whole organism has been subjected during the past few months, but dazzled by the thought that everything is already behind him. When a prisoner walks between the bunks without saying a word to anyone, it is easy for the others to guess that he is a convalescent with rapidly healing scars and a newly-assembled personality, taking his first uncertain steps in a new world."

True, Gustav Herling was able to preserve his remarkable humanity through his ordeals and later was able to express those ordeals with his gift for beautiful expression. But that is not why 'A World Apart' is an important book. It is so because it explains to us, in rather tortuous detail, exactly the process by which human beings were reduced to nothing and then rebuilt into something even less. End of story.

My copy of Primo Levi's 'Survival in Auschwitz' proclaims that it is "a lasting testament to the indestructibility of the human spirit." Primo Levi was a remarkable and brave man and his writings are a gift, if from hell. But the last several sentences of 'Survival in Auschwitz' read:

> Because we also are broken, conquered: even if we know how to adapt ourselves, even if we have finally learnt how to find our food and to resist the fatigue and cold, even if we return home.
>
> We lifted the menaschka on to the bunk and divided it, we satisfied the daily ragings of hunger, and now we are oppressed by shame.

Primo Levi's book is not about the 'indestructibility of the human spirit' but about its destructibility. Levi's book is about how we can adapt to that destructibility, even in our shame, even in our recognition that we can be made into slaves in a heartbeat.

Finally, my copy of Imre Kertész's 'Fatelessness' carries, in a quote from The Washington Times, the claim that the book is "an ornate and honest testimony to the human spirit." That's simply insane actually and probably the result of a time-squeezed reviewer never having bothered to read the book. The reviewer simply saw that it was a novel by an Auschwitz survivor and assumed it could be described as a 'testimony to the human spirit'. And that's the problem in a nutshell. Nothing about the civilization behind wire is a testimony to the human spirit, except, perhaps, in being a testimony to the fact that the human spirit can be crushed into dust more quickly and efficiently and devastatingly than we ever wanted to believe.

Among the many virtues of Imre Kertész's novel is the extent to which he allows himself, through what amount of mental effort we can only imagine, to portray the civilization behind wire as something that has become natural to those who inhabit it, as just another way that human beings live. Here is his description of an evening at Auschwitz:

> Here and there, more suspect plumes of smoke mingled with more benign vapors, while a familiar-sounding clatter drifted up faintly my way from somewhere, like bells in dreams, and as I gazed down across the scene I caught sight of a procession of bearers, poles on shoulders, groaning under the weight of steaming cauldrons, and from far off I recognized, there should be no doubting it, a whiff of turnip soup in the acrid air. A pity, because it must have been that spectacle, that aroma, which cut through my numbness to trigger an emotion, the growing waves of which were able to squeeze, even from my dried-out eyes, a few warmer drops amid the dankness that was soaking my face. Despite all deliberation, sense, insight, and sober reason, I could not fail

to recognize within myself the furtive and yet—ashamed as it might be, so to say, of its irrationality—increasingly insistent voice of some muffled craving of sorts: I would like to live a little bit longer in this beautiful concentration camp.

The implication of that sentence "I would like to live a little bit longer in this beautiful concentration camp" and the tortuous way that the sentence is finally squeezed out of the barely comprehensible experience that elicited it, is the very essence of the literature of the civilization behind wire. I can't blame anyone for not wanting to think that sentence through, to ponder how it could have been uttered and what it means that it was. But, there we are. The civilization behind wire did exist and it has left to us a legacy. I very much wish this weren't the case. But it is.

Morgan Meis

A bare tree in winter, anonymous

Winter

It is a time of dreariness and decay. I'm speaking of winter, of course. I always think, when thinking of winter, of the opening lines of Richard III. Richard, the king-to-be, is musing upon the ascension to the throne of his brother, Edward IV. He says, in lines that are burned into the deep pathways of our neural networks, "Now is the winter of our discontent / Made glorious summer by this son of York."

These opening lines of the play are actually quite hopeful. The first word, "now," looks forward to the "made" in the next line. Shakespeare, in that clever way of his, makes the language fresh by making you pay attention. The "now" is a placeholder for the thought to come. It sets the scenario, grabs us with its immediacy, and lingers there for a moment while we wait for the thought to develop. The thought develops into the idea that "now" is being "made glorious summer" by this son of York. The winter of our discontent is in the past. Now is, in fact, a time of glorious summer, a renewal brought about by the reign of Edward IV, son of York.

But the phrase "now is the winter of our discontent" is so powerful that it often gets picked out of context and made to stand alone. When you do that, it seems as if "now" is the winter of our discontent. The winter of our discontent isn't going anywhere. It is simply the way it is right now.

Sometimes when I hear that line I even hear it as a statement not about "now" but about winter. If you think of it as a winter statement, you can almost replace the word "now" with the word "winter" i.e., "winter is the winter of our discontent." I don't take this as a simple tautology, "winter is winter," but the equation of winter the season with winter the mood. Winter, the season, is a time of general discontent. Winter, in its dreariness and decay, is the season of wanting things to be otherwise.

And yet, some part of us wants winter, some part of us glories in the winteriness of winter. Some part of me does, anyway. I was raised in the perennially pleasant environs of Los Angeles but moved, at eighteen years of age, to New York City, where I've been ever since. I did it partly for the weather. I wanted to experience the seasons. I remember telling people that explicitly, even as a young man. I felt that I was going to gain something important in experiencing a genuine cycle of four seasons. I don't think I knew what I meant by that. But I used to love it when it would rain in Los Angeles. I felt that the city was made suddenly reflective by the rain, that it was being coated in another, deeper layer of what it was by the falling moisture. It made me sad and that pleased me. It was a moment of relief from what I took to be the exhausting project of pretending to be happy all of the time. That is probably an unfair and clichéd accusation against the City of Angels. Still, I felt that way. I loved the rain in Los Angeles and the rain pushed me east. The rain gave me a taste for winter and I went looking for the season of our discontent. I found it, too.

Is there, then, a contentedness in our discontent? There didn't seem to be any for our eloquent hunchback. The second brilliant thing about Shakespeare's opening lines for Richard III is that they set up the theme of the whole play. Although, grammatically speaking, it is the case that Richard is claiming that the winter of our discontent is over and that glorious summer has been achieved, he doesn't really feel that way. In a way, the decontextualized and incorrect interpretation of the first line of the play is the deeper one. Now is the winter of Richard's discontent. He is not, in fact, happy about his brother's ascension to the throne. It vexes and tantalizes him. In fact, Richard wants to be king. He will do anything to achieve that desire, driven as he is by the feeling that his malformations of body have made him a wretched and despised figure. His revenge upon the world will be to rule it. He causes his own brother to be murdered. He litters the play with deceit and treachery. He kills and kills to have his way. In the end, pitifully, he would exchange his entire kingdom for a horse, for the chance to flee, for an escape from the discontent that has driven him ever onward into the pit of doom.

Petulant and resentful, Richard lets loose with one of the more pointed explanations of his devilish ways to be found in the literary record. He says:

Why, I, in this weak piping time of peace,
Have no delight to pass away the time,
Unless to spy my shadow in the sun
And descant on mine own deformity:
And therefore, since I cannot prove a lover,
To entertain these fair well-spoken days,
I am determined to prove a villain

And hate the idle pleasures of these days.

I understand Richard's hatred of "the idle pleasures of these days." They do not seem real to him, those idle pleasures. He feels that the idle pleasures of others mock his own suffering. The lingering discontent in all experience makes him crazy with rage. He would rather destroy the possibility of happiness for everyone than simply let things be. His own deformities have given him a glimpse of something intolerable at the heart of all experience, a shadow that lingers at the edge of the light.

Maybe it is death that tortures him, I don't know. Maybe the discontent that comes to us in winter is in the realization that every moment of joy is but a brief resting point on the greater journey toward oblivion. Or maybe that's too grand. Maybe the discontent in winter is the discontent about the fleeting quality of the present. Nothing holds still for very long, after all. Nothing that feels good stays good for very long. Even in Los Angeles, the perfect sunny day turns to night; a feeling of contentment is replaced by anxiety somewhere along the line.

If there is a greater contentment to be found, then, it is in the contentment of discontent. It is in the willingness, maybe, to have your winters and to have them in their dreariness and decay, neither surrendering completely to that discontent nor pretending to solve it. The cycle of the seasons is, after all, utterly pointless. It just goes round and round. I do not think any meaning can be found in stepping outside of that cycle to explain its purpose from afar. Winter can't be made glorious, can't be transformed into endless summer.

I drove on an empty road just south of Albany the other

day early in the morning. Moisture had frozen on the barren branches of the trees. My feet were cold and the joints in the upper part of my legs were throbbing painfully. I find that happening sometimes in the winter as I get older. A wind blew up from the Hudson River and the flaky slivers of ice were dislodged from the tops of the trees. The slivers fell to the ground slowly, twirling strings of tinsel glinting in the sun. Sharp daggers of light falling across the blue and the white. I was hungry and my jaw muscles were tensed up from a night of grinding my teeth through unremembered dreams. I don't think I will ever forget the icy tinsel in the morning light during this, the 38th winter of my discontent.

Fantasy Sci-fi photo compilation, anonymous

Ruins

Everybody is talking about ruins these days. That could be a bad sign. Detroit, in particular, seems to have captured the fancy of the ruin enthusiast. Detroit has experienced a 25% reduction in population over the last ten years or so. Whole areas of the city have been abandoned. You can see entire neighborhoods in ruin, skyscrapers in ruin, a vastly depopulated downtown area. Camilo José Vergara, a photographer specializing in urban decay, once suggested in the mid-1990s that large sections of downtown Detroit be turned into a "skyscraper ruins park." It would be a testimonial to a lost age, preserved in stone and metal and glass. Today, people sometimes travel to places like Detroit and other Rust Belt locations for the sole reason of gazing upon the ruins.

There have been the dissenters, too, the people who do not take or do not want to take aesthetic pleasure in industrial and urban ruins. The phrase "ruin porn" has made its way into popular parlance. Noreen Malone wrote a piece for The New Republic this year about our love of pictures of the abandoned streets and buildings of Detroit. She argued:

These indelible pictures present an un-nuanced and static vision of Detroit. They might serve to "raise awareness" of the Rust Belt's blight, but raising awareness is only useful if it provokes a next step, a move toward trying to fix a problem. By presenting Detroit, and other hurting cities like it, as places beyond repair, they in fact quash any such instinct.

Malone is right about one thing: the photographs by Vergara do not suggest a next step. Photographs by Yves Marchand and Romain Meffre (who took pictures of Detroit for a traveling exhibition entitled "The Ruins of Detroit") portray an inexorable process of decline. Marchand and Meffre's photograph of an interior of the Woodward Avenue Presbyterian Church, for instance, suggests something post-apocalyptic. Books are strewn across the top of a wobbly piano. Bits of mortar and dust cover what was, not so long ago, finely polished woodwork. It seems as if people left this place suddenly and amidst some catastrophe, never to return. These photos, and the plethora of amateur ruin documentation to be found on the internet, are not created so much out of the need to raise consciousness as out of the need to stand before these ruins in awe. It isn't clear what you do next, after awe. The only thing that is clear from these photos is that the way forward is not clear. From the perspective of the ruin, the future always lacks clarity for the simple reason that ruins look mostly backward.

Having spent some time in Northern Europe last year, I can say that this problem is not isolated to the American Rust Belt. A swath of ruined cities and landscapes stretches from the Ruhr valley in Germany, across Holland and Northern Belgium, up through cities like Manchester in England, and then, skipping over the pond, renewing its rusty march across America's North East before reaching its terminus somewhere in western Illinois.

Another way to put this would be to say that a large geographical portion of Western Civilization currently lies in ruin. Industry, as we all know, has moved elsewhere, to the global south, mostly to China. Industrial civilization as the West has known it from the beginning of the Industrial Revolution sometime in the late 18th century until sometime a few decades ago, is no more. We have been aware of this for some time. We've talked about it frequently. People have written books and articles. Studies have been commissioned. Politicians have made speeches. Some would like to reverse the trend. Others see it as a foregone conclusion. But the basic facts have been known and understood for many years now.

And yet, the ruins are still surprising. They are shocking and terrifying and beautiful and sad. It is one thing to read a paper or to attend a conference in which learned studies about post-industrial society are learnedly discussed. It is another thing to drive around the outskirts of Charleroi, in North West Belgium, where one brick factory building after another fades away into the forest greenery like a medieval castle going to pot in one of the less traveled corridors of the Loire Valley. As you stand near a pool of fetid water outside one of these crumbling factories you realize that the era of the Industrial Revolution (at least in this part of the world) is truly dead, never to be recovered. It is, thus, possible to visit the Rust Belt with the same mood one would visit the chateaus of France or the medieval cities of Spain. You are looking at the remains of a civilization that has passed away. We are not ready, perhaps, to think about visiting Detroit in the same way that we would visit the Palais des Papes in Avignon. But what, really, is the difference?

***

The contemporary artist most associated with ruins is probably Anselm Kiefer. He was born into a ruin, after all. That's to say, he was born in Germany in 1945. He was born into a place that had just been bombed to smithereens from the air and then smashed apart at the ground level by the Allied advance on one side and the Red Army advance on the other. Kiefer's paintings and sculptures reflect a sensibility that was forged during the breaking and smashing of things and then further shaped in an environment where one wandered through the wreckage.

Kiefer works with dirt and broken glass. He likes rusty metal. He paints in streaks of black and grey and in clumps of color that go on the canvas to rot. In a scene near the beginning of Sophie Fiennes' recent movie about Anselm Kiefer (Over Your Cities, Grass Will Grow), we find the artist throwing dust and dirt over a large grey painting depicting forlorn tree trunks in a forest nearby. The entire painting, which must be somewhere in the range of 10' x 20', is covered and then shaken with the help of crane and forklift. It is, literally, unearthed from the rubble.

The rest of Fiennes' film is a lingering meditation on the spaces of Kiefer's longtime studio complex in Barjac, France, which he has recently abandoned for another site. During his many years there, Kiefer dug underground tunnels, deposited paintings and sculptures in rooms left over from the dilapidated silk factory that once existed there, burned things, forged giant books with blank lead pages, and otherwise constructed a landscape of ruin from his own imaginings.

The last scenes of the movie show Kiefer in the midst of directing the building of a series of concrete towers, many of them multiple stories in height. They are constructed in the haphazard manner in which you might build a tower out of playing cards, except using giant blocks of concrete. The towers totter and veer in all directions, some propped up with the giant lead books that Kiefer has been making for years. The result is a mini city of ruins. It is a city not of this time, or of any recent time. In fact, though the teetering towers are made of concrete and lead, they seem to have been brought onto the earth from olden times, maybe the oldest times.

Kiefer himself relates the towers not to anything in our contemporary experience but to biblical stories. That is where the title of the film comes in. "Over your cities, grass will grow," is something, Kiefer tells us, that was said by the biblical character Lilith. In fact, Lilith does not appear in the Bible, but there are Talmudic and other stories about Lilith as a first wife of Adam, before Eve, who quarrels with Adam and leaves him, to become a kind of witch or demon who plagues mankind. In many of the tales, Lilith kills children. Sometimes, she seduces men in order to have their children and then to kill those same children. She is a figure of devastation and barrenness. As the flip side to the story of growth and fecundity (be fruitful and multiply), Lilith gives personification to the sense of futility embedded in all human affairs.

***

We don't talk about it very much, but the unspoken assumption about contemporary civilization is that it will never go completely to ruin. We acknowledge that many past civilizations met exactly such a fate, that over their cities, grass did grow. But things are different now. Certainly we have worried, in decades past, about nuclear annihilation and the devastation it would bring. Currently, we worry about environmental sustainability and global warming. Haunting thoughts of the apocalypse linger in the social imagination. But the dominant thought is one of an endless moving forward through time that is always the same.

That is why Kiefer's structures are so strange and alluring. Where do they come from? What do they point to? How are they able to step outside of the structure of time and the experiences of daily life that the rest of us inhabit?

***

Much merriment was recently had throughout contemporary civilization when Mr. Harold Camping of Family Radio proclaimed the end of the world on May 21st, 2011. The day came and went. Time churned on exactly as it had before. Everyone's expectations about the world's continuity, except those of the followers of Mr. Camping, were confirmed. There was now an opportunity to wag fingers, draw moral lessons about the dangers of fundamentalist thinking, and have a laugh or two.

But was there something else to all the laughter? The obsession with Camping seemed out of all proportion. Why did his proclamation so easily catch our attention? It was almost as if we were all using the opportunity of Camping's crazy prediction in order to experience our own interruption from the usual cycle of time. Talking about how some crazy person had predicted the end of time became an exciting event in itself. Living through the experience of the world not ending had its own exhilaration. We all piggybacked, you might say, on the bold insanity of Camping and his followers in order to indulge some impulse that lurks deep within, some half-understood intuition that there may be a different ordering of time, or that there could be, or that there should be some radical break.

It was simultaneously troubling and amusing to hear about the followers of Camping who had liquidated their assets, gotten rid of all material possessions in order to prepare for The Rapture. Countless news stories focused on the utter absurdity and self-destruction of such actions. Was there also, though, a fascination with such actions? To ridicule others for getting rid of their material possessions is to admit, at the same time, that one's own life is defined and determined by those same possessions. These people were, after all, in their foolish actions, proving that it is possible for something to matter more than material comfort, income, possessions, dry goods. These people believed, genuinely believed, that the world was going to end and that they were going to be judged. Many of them, in the face of such judgment, gave everything away. The last thing they wanted to be tainted by, in the Great Judgment To Come, were all the shiny new things that define so much of our daily activity.

On the final day they were all left standing among the ruins of the lives they had led. They were left with scraps. They had become unworldly, like the lonely tunnels and broken ruins of Anselm Kiefer's compound in Barjac. They had been visited by Lilith, given a glimpse of a different order of time. Those people are living ruins now, a strange testimonial to an alternate logic. Ripped out of the temporal continuum, they are here, but they are not here. Many of them will surely find their way back to the world that the rest of us know. Some, perhaps, will not. Our time will not be able to hold them anymore. The grass is growing upon them.

Morgan Meis

17th Century Archive Sketch, Hudson River

The Hudson River

They call it the Hudson River because of Henry Hudson, the son-of-a-bitch who explored its waters on a mission for the Dutch East India Company. That was four hundred years ago in 1609. Sitting on the upstairs deck of my sister's house in New Baltimore, four hundred years doesn't seem like much. The water is swirling in the thin late-summer light. A thousand years could have passed just now. A million creatures could have died and been born along the shores. A hawk bullets down and shrieks at the water, "Give me fish." The water doesn't care. A barge ambles into the scene, all red rust and splashy wake. Huge. Bigger than seems possible. The river and the trees and the houses say one scale, the barge says another. But the river holds it. The river passes it along.

Henry Hudson spent most of his time looking for the Northwest Passage. He wanted to get through all the pesky land and make it from one ocean, the Atlantic, to another, the Pacific. Such a passage doesn't really exist. To get around North America you've got to do just that, go up and around the thing altogether. But Henry didn't know that. He hoped the river was the ticket, west meets east.

When you're looking for something that bad it screws your brain up. Some suspect that's what happened to Henry. The Northwest Passage drove him crazy. He pushed his crew too far. He couldn't stop and everyone else wanted to go home. Finally, the crew put Henry in a dingy with his son and a few others and set him loose in northern waters. It was mutiny. Real, honest-to-goodness mutiny. Nobody ever saw Henry Hudson again, at least that we know of. He died for the Northwest Passage and for being a stubborn bastard and for not knowing when it is time to go home.

The Hudson River is similarly possessed of an irresponsible flow. It doesn't know whether it is coming or going. That's why the Iroquois and other Native American tribes called it Muhheakantuck, or variations on that. It means "river that flows both ways." Sometimes the Hudson flows north, sometimes it flows south. The water is all mixed up, fresh and salty at the same time. So it's a tricky river, never exactly what it seems, never doing what you think it should.

There's a town called Hudson not too far up the Hudson River that's mixed up just like the river. The central thoroughfare in the town is called Warren Street. It is filled, these days, with high-end antique shops and nice restaurants. The rest of the town is what we used to call a ghetto. You only have to walk one block to get from the high-end part of the town to the ghetto, maybe less. Just step off of Warren Street to enter the heart of 1970s-era urban blight. You can time travel in Hudson, New York using just your feet. You can travel from one America to the other, and they are both strange.

The poet John Ashbery lives in Hudson sometimes. He wrote a confusing poem once called "They Dream Only of America" that may or may not have something to do with

Hudson.

Now he cared only about signs.
Was the cigar a sign?
And what about the key?
He went slowly into the bedroom.
"I would not have broken my leg if I had not fallen
Against the living room table. What is it to be back
Beside the bed? There is nothing to do
For our liberation, except wait in the horror of it.

I do not, myself, know whether the cigar is a sign or the key is a sign, but that's definitely the kind of poem a person would write while living in Hudson. There's a lot of waiting for nothing in Hudson and a lot of signs that don't point anywhere. It's a Hudson poem, with its twists and breaks and backward flowing.

The way I get to Hudson is over the Rip Van Winkle Bridge. It isn't much as far as bridges go. Long and thin, it spans a part of the river that moseys along without the fuss of, say, the Palisades further to the south. But it's the perfect fit for the river: gray, ripple, gray and the green branchy green of the shore and then the roll of the mountains. The funniest thing about the bridge is that it gives up on being cantilevered halfway through and becomes a truss span. So, the Rip Van Winkle is two bridges, really, meeting in confusion at the center of the river.

Rip Van Winkle, as you may recall, was a Catskill Mountain codger who fell asleep for twenty years, mostly to escape his wife's nagging. Funny liquor is what did it to him. The way Washington Irving (himself a Hudson River man) tells the story, it was a group of sailors from Henry

Hudson's crew that gave Rip the bad hooch. They still play their roll, it seems, tricksters on a tricky river.

The Rip Van Winkle Bridge goes from the Catskill side of the Hudson on the west, over to the Hudson side of the river on the east. If you're driving from the west to the east via the Rip Van Winkle there is one structure that will catch your notice without fail. That's Olana, the Persian mansion built by Frederic Edwin Church of the famed Hudson River School of landscape painting.

Frederic was every bit the dreamer old Rip was. He lived in the Hudson Valley but his mind was all over the place. When he wasn't traveling to Ecuador or the Middle East he was conjuring up fantastic visions of the tropics. He surely painted Cotopaxi (one of his most famous paintings) in a fever dream. There's a volcano and a burning yellow sun and waterfalls that disappear into the middle of everything.

I suppose Henry Hudson would have understood Church in his longing for new worlds. A literal man, Hudson looked for the Northwest Passage in actual geography. By Church's time, the Hudson River had been fully charted and explored. But it was still drawing dreamers. The river became an idea generator. Frederic Church was obsessed with Alexander von Humboldt and other European Romantics. The grandeur of nature was, for him, the passage between the physical and the spiritual, matter and mind: Humboldt was looking for the Northwest Passage of the imagination. He worked himself up into a frenzy one day and wrote the following:

> We find even among the most savage nations (as my own travels enable me to attest) a certain vague, terror-stricken sense of the all-powerful unity of natural forces, and of the existence of an invisible, spiritual essence manifested in

these forces, whether in unfolding the flower and matur-
ing the fruit of the nutrient tree, in upheaving the soil of
the forest, or in rending the clouds with the might of the
storm. We may here trace the revelation of a bond of union,
linking together the visible world and that higher spiritual
world which escapes the grasp of the senses.

That's not a bad way to describe what it is like to sit by
the banks of the Hudson. There sure is something about
the Hudson River and evening light. It's like the one was
made for the other and vice versa. We know from physics
that light just shines, acting now like a wave, now like a
particle. That's all it does. But it lays down on the eddies
of the Hudson like a blanket too, catching gleams, throwing out glimmers. It folds the trees up in green with the
orangey reds of early Fall color and presents all that to the
sky. The light has come here just for that, and the Hudson
River is flowing by only to give itself over to the light's play,
and everything is humming along together with a sound
that cannot be heard but vaguely in a whisper at the very
corner of your mind. Hudson's River is four hundred years
old tonight. It is much older by other names and older
by countless millennia from before there were names at
all. But it doesn't seem to mind one bit being the Hudson
River right now.

Section of Francis Bacon's "Head VI," 1948

Francis Bacon

Francis Bacon is a scream. He will always be a scream. Just think of the roar from that fleshy maw under the umbrella in Painting, from 1946. Bacon didn't just paint screams. There are "religious" triptychs, portraits, angry animals, and the ongoing presence of raw meat. But Bacon would not be Bacon without the screams. How you feel about the screams is, I think, the essence of how you'll feel about every Bacon work.

And the man—whose most influential paintings now date back more than half a century—can still stir things up. The current exhibit at the Metropolitan Museum of Art, "Francis Bacon: A Centenary Retrospective," has inspired the full gamut of critical response. People are falling over themselves just to disagree. Jerry Saltz, of New York Magazine, likes the early work and the screaming but thinks Bacon became a parody of himself over time. Saltz writes, "But in the end, he seems less a modern painter than the last of a breed of Romantics—one who, in his final interview, plaintively stated, 'I painted to be loved'."

Roberta Smith over at The New York Times takes the opposite view. Smith dismisses the early work, focusing on the greater emotional complexity of the later paintings. "Yet the Met's exhibition disputes the notion that Bacon's art declined, indicating that it often improved as his colors brightened, his paint handling gained muscularity. It was equally important that he began to focus on people he knew and cared about, giving them faces that seem simultaneously masked, gouged out of wet clay and recognizably individual."

Peter Schjeldahl at The New Yorker gives Bacon grudging respect for being a major artist of the 20th century, but admits that he can't stand the work on any personal level. "Francis Bacon has long been my least favorite great painter of the twentieth century. My notes from a visit to the new Bacon retrospective, which is very handsomely installed at the Metropolitan Museum, seethe with indignation, which I will now try to get over."

I focus here on the critical disparity and unease for one simple reason. It shows the deep distrust in which Bacon is held by those who think and write about art. This distrust, I pose, can be traced back to the scream. Critics tend not to believe in the scream. They think they're being manipulated and they don't like it. Nobody likes to be a sucker, critics least of all. The more the critics witness the public's adoration of Bacon's work, the more they smell a rat.

Arthur Danto, writing on Bacon for The Nation back in 1990, summed up the feelings with his typical intellectual incisiveness.

> So ... these depicted screams seem to entitle us to some inference that they at least express an attitude of despair or outrage or condemnation, and that in the medium of extreme gesture the artist is registering a moral view toward the conditions that account for scream upon scream upon scream. How profoundly disillusioning it is then to read

the artist saying, in a famous interview he gave to David Sylvester for The Brutality of Fact: Interviews with Francis Bacon, "I've always hoped in a sense to be able to paint the mouth like Monet painted a sunset." … It is like a rack maker who listens to the screams of the racked only as evidence that he has done a fine job…. We are accordingly victims ourselves, manipulated in our moral being by an art that has no such being. It is for this reason that I hate Bacon's art.

There is nothing worse, in Danto's eyes, than a scream that means nothing. It amounts to the destruction of the moral realm in the name of aesthetics. The key scream painting in Bacon's oeuvre is probably Study after Velazquez (1950). Bacon takes Velazquez' famous Portrait of Pope Innocent X (1650) in which the Pope is a study in cynicism and power, and transforms it into one of his blurred, terrifying, screaming heads. The impulse is always to explain this, and other screams, through personal history or politics. Bacon was reacting to the horror of his times. Bacon was reacting to the horror of his family life and his later relationships (with their sometimes violent and destructive characteristics). Bacon was reacting to the repressive atmosphere in England regarding his homosexuality. Danto, I think, is correct in rejecting this kind of reductionism. So was Bacon. When asked about his interest in Velasquez' famous Pope painting, Bacon replied, "I think it's the magnificent color of it." He also stated flatly that, "I have never tried to be horrific." Danto can never forgive Bacon for this sleight of hand.

But Danto andmany other critics miss a key distinction when they focus on the meaninglessness of the screams. Bacon retreated to the language of pure painting and aestheticism in order to resist the specific meanings often attributed to his works. None of his paintings were explicitly about the wars and genocides of the 20th century. His Pope paintings are not a criticism of the Catholic Church. His more abstract screams are not an expression of Existentialist philosophy.

In fact, Bacon constantly decontextualized his screams (and other portrayals of violence and terror) in order to cut the causal links and to make the screams more general. He was interested in the form and structure of a scream. He wanted to figure out what makes a scream a scream. Painting the scream onto Pope Innocent X heightens that sense of disjunction. It doesn't make sense that the Pope is screaming. But that makes the scream all the more pure, all the more screamy in its screaminess.

In the aforementioned interview with David Sylvester, Sylvester asks Bacon about the prevalence of violence in his work. Bacon responds with a disturbing account of the ways that, since a small child, he had been constantly surrounded by violence and war. He ends by observing, rather laconically, "So I could say, perhaps, I have been accustomed to always living through forms of violence." It's the way that he calls it "forms of violence" that jumps out at me. The artist in Bacon responded to the specific experience of violence by stepping back and exploring the forms of violence as such. In its structure, this is not unlike many of the abstract painters who were his contemporaries. They stepped back from specific acts of representation in order to study the form of visual perception itself.

It is still possible to accuse Bacon of being blithe and cynical in exploring the forms of violence on one hand while tweaking our ingrained emotional response to images of violence and terror on the other. He is having his cake and eating it too. That's the essence of Danto's critique. Bacon hits us with these incredibly powerful and moving images and then claims, la di da, that he was only interested in the color orange all along.

But why shouldn't artists get to explore the forms of violence just as they explore all other forms? With all due respect to Edvard Munch, I can't think of another artist who so perfectly expressed the Platonic purity of the scream, the scream as scream. There are plenty of artists who exploit our specific attraction to beautiful bodies or landscapes in order to explore more general aesthetic questions about shape, or color, or beauty itself.

Something about Bacon's exploitation of horror arouses an indignation not usually expressed in these other cases. Perhaps we resent that Bacon makes us take pleasure in our more troubling emotions, in our fascination with violence. I don't know if Peter Schjeldahl "seethes with indignation" because he deplores the amorality of Bacon's imagery of violence or because he deplores the pleasure he finds himself taking in such amoral imagery of violence. It could be a mixture of both.

I always take very seriously the way that teenagers look at Bacon. They see the purity of that scream and they respond to it immediately. They know that it is right, that Bacon got that scream absolutely right exactly because he formalized the subject matter and not because it points to any outside meaning. They stand before those paintings in an open display of their own essential desire, revulsion, lust, anger, fear. There it is. Scream.

Moby-Dick, Classic Comics illustration, 1950s

Moby Dick

Moby-Dick is not about Moby-Dick. Not really. The white whale makes his appearance, of course. We have been promised that much. Moby-Dick emerges, finally, at the end of Melville's great novel, in the deepest part of the Pacific Ocean. "There she blows!—there she blows! A hump like a snow-hill! It is Moby-Dick!" The white whale comes out of the sea in order to do battle with his human nemesis, Captain Ahab. An encounter with Moby-Dick on a previous whaling expedition left Ahab without one leg, shorn off by the massive sperm whale's prodigious jaw. Ahab's crazed obsession with finding and killing Moby-Dick becomes the guiding obsession for the entire book. Everyone aboard Ahab's ship, the Pequod, slowly gets pulled into Captain Ahab's obsession. But no one ever understands it. Not really. No one aboard the Pequod, not Ishmael the narrator, or Queequeg the harpoonist, or Starbuck the first mate, is ever sure why they seek the white whale across the seven seas. "Oh, my Captain! my Captain!" cries Starbuck, "why should anyone give chase to that hated fish! Away with me! let us fly these deadly waters! let us home!" Captain Ahab understands it least of all, this obsession. "Is

Ahab, Ahab?" he asks, "Is it I, God, or who, that lifts this arm?" Ahab has moved beyond just having an obsession; he is the obsession.

But it is not really Moby-Dick that drives them all out onto the open seas. It is something bigger, even, than a whale. Moby-Dick and Ahab are but creaturely manifestations of the more infinite subject of Herman Melville's inquiry: the ocean. In a sense, Melville was writing to the ocean and he was trying to let the ocean speak back. The conversation starts in the opening pages of Moby-Dick as Ishmael is drawn outward and away from the land, into the nameless blue from the island of Manhattan, an island that, for Melville, was but a launching point for journeys into the sea.

Look out at the island of the Manhattoes, Melville writes in Moby-Dick, and what do you see?

> Posted like sentinels all around the town, stand thousands upon thousands of mortal men fixed in ocean reveries. Some leaning against the spiles, some seated upon the pier-heads; some looking over the bulwarks of ships from China; some high aloft in the rigging, as if striving to get a still better seaward peep.

But what does a man peep into when he makes his seaward peep? What is out there? What is it that gets glimpsed when there is no land to be found and everything on all sides is but ocean and sky? Ishmael says it in the pages of Moby-Dick: "in landlessness alone resides the highest truth, shoreless, indefinite as God." You want to get a seaward peep because you want to get a glimpse of the truth.

During Melville's time, the mid-nineteenth century, the boundlessness of the sea, the infinity of it, was, perhaps, its primary characteristic. The whaling industry—the industry that makes Melville's tale possible—had become big business. Mankind was beginning, in full earnest, to tap into the resources of the great oceans. But the tap seemed only to touch upon the barest surface of an unfathomable depth. That word comes up a lot, 'unfathomable'. Cannot be fathomed. A fathom is six feet, two yards. The original standard for its measurement, we're told, was roughly the length, from fingertip to fingertip, of a normal-sized man's outstretched arms. When you talk about something being unfathomable, then, you are talking about something impossible for human beings to get their arms around. It is bigger than our grasp.

The highest truth is therefore going to be out there on the oceans, where the sightline stretches out into a shoreless infinity and the depth below you is unknowable, "indefinite as God." The highest truth is going to stretch the very possibility of our fathoming by the very nature of its being the highest truth. It is going to outstretch the grasp. That is what Melville sees in our collective drive to get a seaward peep. We have a desire to get beyond ourselves, to the point at which our capacity to understand would almost snap.

This is something that Charles Olson noticed about Herman Melville and about Moby-Dick, too. Olson considers it particularly American, this obsession with space and with depth in its limitless expanse—the terrifying indefiniteness. "I take SPACE to be the central fact to man born in America, from Folsom cave to now. I spell it large because it comes large."

Olson wrote that in Call me Ishmael. Charles Olson—critic, poet, and central figure of the Black Mountain school in the 1950s—published his book in 1947, adapted from a dissertation he wrote on Melville and Shakespeare. Olson's big idea was that there were two versions of Moby-Dick. The first was a tale of the sea that did not include the character of Ahab. The second, the one we all know, includes Ahab and came about after Melville read a lot of Shakespeare, notably King Lear, who Melville fell in love with as a character that speaks a "madness of vital truth." In reading Shakespeare, thinks Olson, Melville understood that his novel had to include the dark element. If the sea is unfathomable and as indefinite as God, the thinking goes, then it must also be as indefinite as Satan. Melville once wrote to his friend Nathaniel Hawthorne that he had written a "wicked book." Olson thinks of the "wicked book" as the Book of Ahab that exists within the pages of the larger work, Moby-Dick. "Melville's 'wicked book,'" Olson says, "is the drama of Ahab, his hot pursuit for the White Whale, and his vengeful pursuit of it from the moment the ship lunges like fate into the Atlantic."

This drama of essential forces and the barely under-standable madness of Ahab can only be written against the backdrop of the open seas because that is the only place big enough, indefinite enough in its cosmic-though-still-worldly significance, to hold such a tale. For Charles Olson, such a tale must be told by an American. That's because America is "geography at bottom, a hell of wide land from the beginning." And it is not just the land, since there are "seas on both sides, no barriers to contain as rest-less a thing as Western man was becoming in Columbus' day. That made Melville's story (part of it)."

It is a point that has been made time and again. The first stories of Western man happen upon a sea that is land enclosed. The civilizations of the Mediterranean Sea look inward by design. Even the word "Mediterranean" says it all: "medius terra," "middle land." The Mediterranean is the sea utterly surrounded and embraced by the land. Olson points to this fact in talking about the trip that Melville took after he finished writing Moby-Dick, the trip he took to see the old civilization around the Mediterranean. "The Mediterranean is a close sea, is in the middle of the land, is the old center of earth." Dangerous as sailing the Mediterranean could be, especially in ancient times, it was nevertheless the exploration of a space that was inherently bounded. Odysseus travels far and wide during his wanderings in The Odyssey, but he always finds something as he bounces from shore to shore. The American experience is one of being opened into shorelessness, either toward the Atlantic and Pacific—oceans that are not enclosed by land—or in the experience of the "hell of wide land" that just seems to keep going and going as American civilization moves west. "The fulcrum of America," writes Olson, "is the Plains, half sea half land, a high sun as metal and obdurate as the iron horizon, and a man's job to square the circle." Melville makes the same point from the opposite direction in Moby-Dick, calling the Pacific a "sea pasture" and discussing the oceans as "wide-rolling watery prairies and Potters' Fields." In so much open space, of land or of water, it is a natural thing to want to get your bearings, to figure out where you are.

Is it any wonder, then, that American literature of the 19th century returns obsessively to space, how to mark it and to take its measure? Mark Twain cast off his given name, Samuel Langhorne Clemens, to take up the name of a depth sounder. The call of "mark twain" was what the leadsman of a riverboat would shout out. It meant that the lead line trailing the boat was showing the second mark, a mark that signified that the water was two fathoms deep. Mark twain is two fathoms deep; it is safe water. That is something a human being can get his arms around, two fathoms. And that is the territory of American literature that Mark Twain staked out for himself. Mark Twain went about two fathoms deep in everything he explored. That was how far he was willing to let his literary imagination go. He explored those two fathoms with great brilliance. He was defined by the Mississippi, which he thought of as the most significant dwelling place for civilized man upon the entire globe. The Mississippi is a meandering river. Twain knew that well. There is a trickiness in navigating her. But there is nothing shoreless about the Mississippi; you can always see from one shore to the other. Maybe the biggest difficulty for river boaters like Samuel Clemens was to make sure that the river didn't get too shallow in parts to navigate. Mark Twain was, thus, always looking for mark twain, the place where there was just enough depth to move around in, but not too much. Twain's humor and warmth is, likewise, always human-sized. He liked the man or the experience that could be fathomed, that he could get his arms around. There are no Ahabs in the writings of Mark Twain. He told Americans about the safe water.

Or think of Henry David Thoreau living on Walden Pond. He lived there and wrote his book in the mid-1800s, within a few years of when Melville wrote Moby-Dick. What did he do? He decided he needed to sound out the depth of Walden Pond. He needed to get the space right and to figure out the distances, to take the measure. Thoreau was amazed by the general lack of curiosity in the depth of the pond. Most people seem to take it as bottomless, unfathomable. "Many have believed that Walden reached quite through to the other side of the globe." But Thoreau does the work of sounding with a cod line and a one-and-a-half-pound stone. He finds that the pond is remarkably deep, though it has a bottom. It is one hundred and two feet deep, and with a rise in the pond of five feet since he did his sounding, one hundred and seven feet deep.

This pleases Thoreau, the idea that Walden Pond is deep, but not too deep to fathom. Thoreau even takes a moment to wonder what it would be like if all ponds were shallow. "Would it not react on the minds of men?" he asks. The thought bothers him. We need depth, he thinks, we need the idea and the experience of depth. "I am thankful that this pond was deep and pure for a symbol," he writes, "While men believe in the infinite some ponds will be thought to be bottomless."

If Mark Twain is the thinker of safe water, then Thoreau is the thinker of hidden depths. He is the American for whom infinity could spiral out from an inch of space, when looked at properly. Thoreau explains it like this:

> Our notions of law and harmony are commonly confined to those instances which we detect; but the harmony which results from a far greater of seemingly conflicting, but really concurring laws, which we have not detected, is still more wonderful. The particular laws are our points of view, as, to the traveler, a mountain outline varies with every step, and it has an infinite number of profiles, though absolutely but one form.

Thoreau had a genius for holding those two perspectives simultaneously. He loved to watch the outline of the mountain in its minute changes as the traveler walks along and the space changes, the light changes, the day transforms.

And he was always able to see that mountain as selfsame in its absolute form. He was a specialist in observing the infinity of particularities without losing himself in the infinity. When Thoreau sounded out Walden Pond, it was to know it in every detail, to run his hand along its topography by means of rock and string. But he had a natural instinct for limits. "Even when cleft or bored through," Thoreau says of his hypothetical mountain, "it is not comprehended in its entireness." And he was content to leave it at that. He was content to wander through the woods of Walden in a never-ending odyssey of discovery. When Thoreau picked up a leaf, he wanted to know what kind of leaf it was, but then he wanted to think about the leaf as something unique too. There was a constant balancing act at play in Thoreau's capacity for observation. He was wary both of the infinity that stretched out forever in the details and of getting lost in the meditation on absolute form. Depth, for Thoreau, was only meaningful when it could be related back to the human scale. There is even a moment in Walden when Thoreau dismisses the idea that the ocean holds any great depth. "Probably," writes Thoreau, "the depth of the ocean will be found to be very inconsiderable compared to its breadth." In one sentence, Thoreau makes the significance of the Pacific Ocean equivalent to that of Walden Pond. And that was how Thoreau liked everything: Walden-sized.

Melville would have lasted about five minutes on Walden Pond. The call of the sea was, to Melville, the call of infinity. But how, then, do you measure the ocean, how do you come to terms with it? In a passage from Melville's travel journal while he was in Egypt, Charles Olson discovers the following lines: "Finding it vain to take in the sea's vastness man has taken to sounding it and weighing its density;

so with the pyramid, he measures the base and computes the size of individual stones. It refuses to be studied or adequately comprehended. It still looms in my imagination, dim and indefinite." On the face of it, these thoughts on the inadequacy of comprehension are not dissimilar from the thoughts on limitation that can be found in Thoreau's musings. The difference is that Melville can't leave it alone. The vastness looms in his imagination, haunting him. Where Thoreau is content in his wonder, Melville is driven on to the core of it, where it burns and festers in his soul.

***

This brings us back to the whale. The whale is the sea's greatest creation. The whale is massive enough, powerful enough, grand enough to seem adequate to the open waters in which it swims. The whale is shoreless, just like the waters it inhabits. That is why a beached whale is so incongruous, so distressing to the head and heart. When a whale ends up on the shore, a cosmic compact has gone awry. Get it back, get it back into the ocean, we think, with an urgency that is all the more galling for how little we understand either the whale or our need to get him off the beach. We only know the whale needs to be in its proper place.

More important than simply being in the waters of the ocean is the specific mode in which whales inhabit those waters. Whales are sounders. They take the depth. They go down and they come up again. There is a straightforward explanation for this behavior. Whales are mammals. They need to breathe in the same air as the rest of us mammals. They come to the surface of the ocean in order to take that air. And then they can go back down into the unknown crevices of the seas. But they must come up, they must come up again. And that is how we get to know them. The entire industry of whaling—the industry that brought Herman Melville into the oceans in the first place—was predicated on the mammalian behavior of the whale. The sounding of the whale and then its return to the surface of the water taught whalers to track and anticipate. The fact that whales exist in two worlds and that one of those worlds is ours, means that we have access to them. Brutally, for all the greatness of the whale, its need to breathe in the same air as man means that it's something we can kill.

It also happens that whales–especially species like the Sperm Whale–are filled with high-quality oil. In the 19th century, in the days before electricity, the oiliness of the whale meant the possibility of light. Lamps all over the world were getting their fuel from the life-essences of whales. These facts–the whale, the oil, the need for light– were the facts that brought Herman Melville, the man, out into the great oceans of the world. And as he experienced whales, as he observed them from the whaling ships on which he traveled, he began to realize that whales were his access to the truth of the ocean just as they were, literally, his reason for sailing the seas. These great beasts were at home in the ocean. They experienced daily, in their sound-ing, the reality of the infinite depths. Just in the way that Thoreau used a cod line and a one-and-a-half-pound stone to feel out the depths of Walden Pond, Melville uses the whale to feel out the ocean in its incomprehensibility. He would know the ocean through the creature that most knows the ocean. He would know the being of the whale, if he could, the soul of the whale, if they had one. He would become an expert of the whale.

In fact, Melville never understood much about whales. He couldn't grasp the whale as a mammal. He mustered all his scientific acumen, such as it was, and definitively proclaimed the whale a fish. Melville writes (in properly playful manner given the dubious grounds for his claim), "Be it known that, waiving all argument, I take the good old fashioned ground that the whale is a fish, and call upon holy Jonah to back me." He merely adds what he considers the important detail of the directionality of its tail. "To be short, then, a whale is a spouting fish with a horizontal tail." So be it.

This passage comes within what many consider the most confusing and off-putting section of Moby-Dick, where Melville makes of his novel a document of mid-19th century naturalism, and not particularly good naturalism at that. It all happens in Chapter 32 of Moby-Dick, titled 'Cetology' (though the naturalist impulse comes back again here and there throughout the middle of the book). Cetology is the study of whales and Melville, via the narrative voice of Ishmael, is eager to delve into its business. "It is some systematized exhibition of the whale in his broad genera," he writes, "that I would fain put before you."

Melville then launches into fifteen pages or so that are, by his own account and by the account of most readers since then, of such little value with regards to science (or the readability of the novel) that it is often considered polite to ignore this part of the book. Not everyone, though, feels this way. The poet Dan Beachy-Quick, for instance, published just last year an intriguing volume entitled A Whaler's Dictionary, inspired specifically by the 'Cetology' chapter.

Beachy-Quick admits that Melville's performance in that

chapter is, "more touching than pedantic." It is a difficult task that Melville set himself since the one thing about whales is that, "they are always diving down." But Beachy-Quick understands Melville's need to define the whale, to catalogue and categorize the whale even if it ends in failure. The whale, as the creature that inhabits the pure world of the ocean as well as the surface world of human beings, is a potential key through which the one world can understand the other. Beachy-Quick says, "The white whale connects surface to depth and, in his strange, alien, inexplicable intelligence, carries knowledge from one world to another." By understanding something about the white whale, then, there is some hope that Melville/Ishmael will have a greater understanding of his own desire to get the seaward peep. "The white whale is a creature capable of living in this hellish night darker than night," Beachy-Quick writes, "but he is also a creature who contains that element that struck by flame turns into flame. Moby-Dick is a wick in the water and so promises, within the complexity of his symbolic nature, to illuminate what before was unlit."

What is it, then, that is illuminated by the sounding of the white whale? What does he bring up for us to know from all the darkness? Meditating on the face of the Sperm Whale in one short chapter of Moby-Dick, Ishmael becomes fascinated by its forehead, comparing it to the foreheads of Shakespeare and Melancthon. "But in the great Sperm Whale," we are told, "this high and mighty god-like dignity inherent in the brow is so immensely amplified, that gazing on it, in that full front view, you feel the Deity and the dread powers more forcibly than in beholding any other object living in nature." And beyond that, words fail him. Ishmael simply cannot explain it any further. "I but put that brow before you," he says, "Read it if you can."

Along those same lines, Beachy-Quick makes an observation in the "Description" entry of his whaler's dictionary. He says:

> The assumption underlying our words is simple: that we speak in order to show meaning. Moby-Dick threatens such inherited notions of language's purpose, language's possibility of meaning. A word, like a whale, dives down. It sounds. The descriptive capacity we profit by when we speak may be but an accidental quality of language's darker, depth-ridden, actual activity.

It is just like a poet to say something like that. It is the poet, after all, who spends the most time with the magical aspects of language, when words and phrases access something more than what is immediately available on the surface. When you work with language closely enough, making it say things, you begin to suspect that there are darker, depth-ridden mysteries to be found there. You begin to suspect that everything we actually say is just a glimmering of what we really mean to say, of what we could be saying if we could only get deep enough. Maybe that is an illusion, a trick that language itself produces in the act of producing meaning. But maybe not. It is, after all, consistently mysterious to linguists, philosophers, and scientists alike, how it is that we human beings smuggle meaning to one another through the utterance of guttural noises.

If nothing else, an abiding and central theme of Moby-Dick is that there are truths and that they are hard to say. The whole reason that Ishmael goes off on his expedition, sails away on the blasted and infernal deck of The Pequod, is to indulge in the full measure of the seaward peep. The seaward peep, Melville explains to us again and again in formulation after formulation (none of which ever seem to fully satisfy him), is looking at the truth unvarnished. But the truth unvarnished is a very difficult thing to look at, partly because it is too big to see, partly because its lack of varnish leaves it without specific contours.

What is the point, you ask, what is the point of all this? Where is all this confusion driving? Why are we out on the oceans at the behest of a madman?

In the face of these questions, Melville always goes back to the beginning, to the desire: we want to get a seaward peep. That is how it all starts. Just remember how Ishmael explains himself at the beginning of Moby-Dick. He tells us why he ventures out to find a whaling ship.

> Chief among those motives was the overwhelming idea of the great whale himself. Such a portentous and myste-rious monster roused all my curiosity. Then the wild and distant seas where he rolled his island bulk; the undeliver-able, nameless perils of the whale; these, with all the attend-ing marvels of a thousand Patagonian sights and sounds, helped to sway me to my wish. ... I am tormented with an everlasting itch for things remote.

If you have ever wanted to get a seaward peep, then you understand. You have itched for the things remote. You need a whale, a messenger from the realm of nameless peril. And then you will be taken to the places that are wild and distant. If there are, still, any places that are wild and distant.

***

Much has changed, of course, since Melville's time. The oceans that we encounter do not, cannot have the same sense of wild, the same feeling of distance that they had one hundred and fifty years ago. But that itch for things remote still exists. The ocean is still held up as a symbol of the vast spaces beyond our ken. Whales, in order to be watched more than to be hunted, still serve as motivation for that itch. But anything will do, any flimsy excuse will suffice if it gets us out into the things remote. For Donovan Hohn (whose contribution to the legacy of Moby-Dick is Moby-Duck: The True Story of 28,800 Bath Toys Lost at Sea and the Beachcombers, Oceanographers, Environmentalists, and Fools, Including the Author, Who Went in Search of Them), the excuse to go out to sea was nothing more than the loss of a few shipping containers of bathtub toys during a storm on January 10th, 1992. The toys began to wash up on shores all over the world. Newspaper and magazine articles started appearing about the rubber duckies that navigated the seven seas. In asking what happened to the toys in their ocean journey, Hohn ends up sailing the oceans and telling a tale of the global economy, manufacturing in China (where the toys were made), of the Great Pacific Garbage Patch (a swirl of marine litter in the North Pacific Ocean somewhere around the size of Texas), our addiction to plastic, and a few other things besides.

At its heart, though, the book is just another man's desire to get a seaward peep. Hohn wanted to get out there and explore the marvels of the Patagonian sights and sounds. Read, for instance, this: "Surveying the colorful, oversize jacket of my atlas, a cartographic wonder made—its dust jacket boasted—from high-resolution satellite photographs and 'sophisticated computer algorithms' ... fantasy did not strike me as extinct, or even remotely endangered. The ocean was far less fathomable to my generation of Americans than it was when Melville explored that 'watery wilderness' a century and a half ago."

It is a fair point, and a tantalizing one. There has been a giant push to chart and graph and measure and fathom the oceans over the time since Melville wrote his book. It happened roughly as Melville suggested it would in his travel journals during his trip to the Pyramids. "Finding it vain to take in the sea's vastness man has taken to sounding it and weighing its density." In the course of sounding the ocean and weighing it, we've discovered that it is a delicate thing, as well. Our industries can change its chemistry. Our activities can determine its contents, what lives and dies, how the waters are populated. The oceans have gone from being what Hohn describes as "indomitable, unfathomable, dangerous, and divine," to what is today "the fragile wonder world of Carson and Cousteau." We have discovered that the oceans are, like everything else in this world, something that we can potentially destroy that we, maybe, are destroying.

But then again, there is a limit to all this sounding, a natural barrier to the knowledge that can be gained from the oceans as a subject of scientific inquiry. The motion of the ocean, it turns out, is infinitely complex, just as Melville always suspected it was. Ishmael muses in Moby-Dick that, "however baby man may brag of his science and skill, and however much, in a flattering future, that science and skill may augment; yet for ever and ever, to the crack of doom, the sea will insult and murder him, and pulverize the stateliest, stiffest frigate he can make." And a version of that prophecy has come to pass. The scientific instruments we've developed to track the data of the oceans have discovered a hitherto unsuspected indeterminacy that seems the very structure of the sea. As Hohn puts it, "The ocean is not so much a place as a kind of weather." That weather is composed of the play of hot and cold water, the swirling of tides and currents and storms upon the ocean's surface. "What we think of as the surface of the sea oceanographers now think of as 'ocean-atmosphere interface', a member more permeable than it looks. ... Map the ocean? You might as well map the clouds!"

Hohn is telling a tale of the contemporary ocean that would seem, on the face of it, to be the tale of a place so charted, so explored, so understood that it bears little resemblance to the place of infinite awe that Melville knew. Yet, Hohn is never able to track down the bath toys, the little Moby Ducks that initially sent him on his journey. There are too many places they could have gone. They could be stuck in the ice somewhere in the Arctic Circle. They could be swirling around in the Great Garbage Patch that is too vast to track in all its particulars. They might have sounded long ago, falling down to the ocean floor anywhere across millions of unmarked acres. The complexity of the ocean and its currents, the fact that mapping it is like mapping the clouds, opens up the realm of infinity again.

You might say that infinity, now, is hidden within the fully charted oceans in the way Thoreau would have appreciated. It is not the brazen outward show that Melville went looking for. But it is there. The mystery is simply folded up instead of laid bare. Donovan Hohn experiences a revelation when he leaves the shore and finds himself upon the open sea. He begins to grasp a truth there in the hidden infinity, in the realm of shorelessness. He sees that the reality we think we know, the everyday reality of the Manhattoes, melts away in the face of that truth. Hohn has been traveling around the Pacific looking for plastic. He says,

> It occurs to me now, as it has before, that this is what I have
> been pursuing these past months, this is what I found so
> spellbindingly enigmatic about the image of those plastic
> ducks at sea—incongruity. We have built for ourselves out
> of this New World a giant diorama, a synthetic habitat, but
> travel beyond the edges or look with the eyes of a serious
> beachcomber and the illusion begins to crumble like flot-
> sam into sand.

That, I think, is a good way to think about the will to
truth that motivates men when they are trying to get their
seaward peep. The truth is not, ultimately, a truth about
the ocean itself. It is an anti-truth. The ocean is everything
that is left when you wipe civilization away completely.
Going out into the ocean is an act of obliteration. The
ocean is so big and so empty that everything has the capacity to crumble in the face of it. It is, then, also like a time
machine, rolling back the story of human history to the
very beginning.

The fact that Moby-Dick is a novel about the ocean as
an "anti-truth" thus makes it a kind of anti-novel. The
great European novels that precede Moby-Dick are often
described as Bildungsromans. We can translate Bildungsro-
man roughly as "formation novel" or "novel of education."
Goethe's Wilhelm Meister is its archetype. In a Bildungsro-
man, we are taken on a story of development. Often, the
story tracks the literal development of a human being from
childhood to adulthood. Or it might tell the story of the
rise of a family over generations. Or the development of
civilization itself.

Melville's novel blasts that process open completely.
Ishmael begins his journey in the heart of American civili-

zation, on the island of Manhattan. But even before he sees the water, he is seized with dissatisfaction. He speaks of a "drizzly November in my soul," of "growing grim about the mouth." In short, Ishmael feels a lack, a discontent. He is driven by something gnawing at him from within. Not so different, in its early stages, from the situation in which Goethe's Wilhelm Meister finds himself after a failed love affair with an actress. The difference is that Wilhelm Meister takes a journey deeper and deeper into the heart of civilization. He discovers genuine civilization hiding within the outward trappings of the superficialities of civilization. Wilhelm Meister, living in Germany at the end of the 19th century, has nowhere else to go, alas, but deeper in. Wilhelm Meister is a landlocked novel.

Ishmael sees things differently. He gets the itch and it makes him want to throw everything away. Civilization must be cast off. The bildungs-process, the development process must be cast aside. He doesn't want it. Ishmael is suddenly tantalized by the idea of open space, by the draw of nothingness. That American possibility of open space, truly open space, makes the impulse toward obliteration a real possibility. He can go out there. Even the density of urban space, the weight of Manhattan is not too strong to keep him. He can arrest the development process right there and go back to the beginning. He can cancel everything and then restart.

On the last page of Wilhelm Meister we find our hero compared to Saul, who went out seeking an ass and found a kingdom. Meister set out in despair, but managed to find his true place in society. "I know not the worth of a kingdom," says Wilhelm, "but I know I have attained a happiness which I have not deserved, and which I would not change with anything in life." On the final page of Moby-Dick, the Pequod is sinking and Ahab is going down to his depths. The last vestige of civilization is being swept away. "Now small fowls flew screaming over the yet yawning gulf; a sullen white surf beat against its steep sides; then all collapsed, and the great shroud of the sea rolled on as it rolled five thousand years ago."

Coming into contact with the open sea is a fundamental act, a mythical act. It renews a man. Or so thought Melville. It makes living on land possible again. According to Charles Olson, Melville once told Hawthorne that he dated his life from his return from the Pacific. He didn't have access to real life until he went out there, until he let the shoreless infinity crumble his illusions like flotsam. Olson says, "We are (inevitably?), as humans, Antaean: only in touch with the land and water of the earth do we keep our WEIGHT, retain POTENTIAL. Melville kept his by way of the Pacific."

The question mark in Olson's quote is telling. We do not know our limits. We cannot know if there is a point at which we have so transformed the oceans that we have transformed ourselves. So, perhaps, all we can do is keep going out there to check, keep trying to get a seaward peep. We haven't forgotten Melville's book yet, which is a sign of something. We are still obsessed with the white whale. We want, like Dan Beachy-Quick and Donovan Hohn, to get a peep just as much as Ishmael ever did. As Thoreau said about his beloved Walden, "While men believe in the infinite some ponds will be thought to be bottomless." Melville believed in the bottomlessness of the oceans, a bottomlessness where "millions of mixed shades and shadows, drowned dreams, somnambulisms, reveries, all that we call lives and souls, lie dreaming, dreaming, still; tossing like slumberers in their beds; the ever-rolling waves but made so by their restlessness," giving us WEIGHT and POTEN-TIAL just as much today as they ever did.

Section of "The Smoker," Frans Hals, 1625

Frans Hals

Frans Hals is often described as a "loose" painter. You can see what that means in one of Hals' great paintings currently on display at the Metropolitan Museum of Art in New York City. The painting is called "The Smoker," from 1625. You wouldn't be surprised, though, if someone told you it was painted 250 years later than that. The face of the young man smoking a pipe at the center of the painting is rendered in almost impressionistic strokes. A dab of red here, a curve of yellow there. The collar of the man's shirt is created with a rough stab of white down the middle of the canvas. The painstaking brushwork of other Dutch masters from the Golden Age is notably absent.

That is not to say Hals was sloppy, a crime for which he has sometimes been accused. Hals labored at his chosen craft all life long. It is just that he worked very hard to achieve a looser style. You can see it even in his formal portraits, in works like "Portrait of a Man" from 1636-8. The face of the man in that painting is rendered with all the precision you might find in a Rubens of roughly the same era. And the expressiveness of the man's face is reminiscent of Rembrandt. But if you look at the man's left arm, the one cocked at his hip, you notice that the style devolves (or evolves?) into that of the loose Hals again. The elbow--and the folds of garment around the elbow--are painted with the same rough gestures and impressionistic swaths of color that are so startling in "The Smoker."

It is sometimes thought that Hals was a man ahead of his time. He never commanded much of a price for his paintings, though he was respected well enough during a life spent in the town of Haarlem in The Netherlands. His paintings were to fall out of what modest fashion they had enjoyed already near the end of his life, when he was left a ward of the state due to his inability to pay his bills. For a century or so, no one wanted his paintings and they could be had at auction for a pittance. It wasn't until the mid-19th century and the birth of Modernism in painting that people really began to appreciate Hals. The Impressionists were excited about his work, particularly that characteristic loose style. Van Gogh was famously amazed by Hals' usage of twenty-seven varieties of the color black.

Still, I would say that it was his timeliness rather than his timelessness that made Hals a great painter. You see, Frans Hals was born of a generation of painters that had been stripped of their subject matter. It is hard, today, to fully understand the significance of that fact, since we take it for granted that paintings can depict anything and that painters are free to explore any subject matter they like.

Frans Hals was born in the late 16th century in Antwerp. Strange and dangerous things were happening in Flanders during those days. A few years before Hals was born, Spanish troops had gone on a rampage through Antwerp killing thousands of citizens in the streets and burning down large chunks of the city. The event has since become known as The Spanish Fury. These were terrible and extraordinary times. The religious wars, kicked off by the Protestant Reformation, were ravaging these lands. The Hapsburg Empire was attempting to hold onto power in the Lowlands. A group of Dutchmen led initially by William of Orange were in open revolt against the Hapsburgs and the Pope.

Frans Hals' father was a Catholic living in Antwerp. A few years after the birth of Frans, and with the upheaval of the ongoing siege of Antwerp, the whole family had moved to Haarlem and become Protestants. They had chosen sides. Frans Hals' more than eighty-year lifespan corresponds very closely to that of The Eighty Years War, a war in which the nascent Dutch Republic struggled to hold its own against the forces of Phillip II and the Counter Reformation. In short, most of Frans Hals' life was spent under the sign of a giant question mark. It was a time of war, the conclusion of which could easily have meant utter destruction for the Dutch cities in revolt. It was a time of revolution in religion, a wholesale remaking of the relationship between man and God. It was a time in which people were forced to question all of their beliefs and allegiances and, in many cases, to begin life anew under circumstances utterly transformed by history. Such was the case for the Hals family.

The Protestant Netherlands that Frans Hals found himself living in at the end of the 16th century as he was just learning about art and painting was a society that had recently seen the destruction of many statues and paintings depicting religious subject matter. This is known as the Beeldenstorm in Dutch (literally the "statue storm"). In English we call it the Iconoclastic Fury. It was inspired by the back-to-basics standpoint of Northern European Protestantism, which had become disgusted with the decadence and "worldliness" of the Catholic Church. The iconoclasts were looking back to the Ten Commandments. The Second Commandment, after all, proclaims that "You shall not make for yourself a graven image, or any likeness of anything that is in heaven above, or that is in the earth beneath, or that is in the water under the earth; you shall not bow down to them or serve them." Many Protestants were suddenly moved to take this Commandment quite seriously. The main church in the city where Hals was born, Antwerp, became a notable victim of the Fury when a mob destroyed much of the interior of the church along with all the art displayed there. People were killed too.

Suffice it to say that if you were making art in the immediate aftermath of the Beeldenstorm, you were doing so with a refreshed understanding of what art can and cannot be about. On one reading of the Second Commandment, there should not be art that contains any images at all. According to more lenient interpretations, the Second Commandment was thought to apply only to works that treated religious matters in such a way as to promote idolatry. Art of a secular nature would be acceptable since non-religious art didn't require that anyone bow down to it or serve it. You could say, then, that it was precisely because of the religious piety of men like Frans Hals that a fully secular art was born.

The art of Frans Hals is something of a grand experiment in non-religious art, though in no way was it an anti-religious art. It is an art that takes the Second Commandment seriously and that, thusly, pays tribute to God and to the religion of Hals' Protestant contemporaries precisely in what it does not depict. There are no saints or martyrs or direct portrayals of biblical scenes in the art of Frans Hals. He was pious by remaining silent, by withholding his brush from such potentially idolatrous subject matter. If he was going to address religious themes, he was going to have to do so in an entirely new way.

But what, then, does a painter paint, and how does he go about painting it? That, I think, was the question Frans Hals was trying to answer in his body of work. It is a question that only makes sense when you see it in the proper context. It has sometimes been suggested, for instance, that Hals was a lover of pubs and prostitutes and debauched living, since he often portrayed such things, especially in his earlier paintings. Frans Hals, so the modern viewer of his work might think, glorified the secular world. He was a kind of painterly polemicist for the separation of Church and State. In fact, no such thing is the case. Hals was trying to bring moral arguments into his depiction of secular scenes just as any religious painter would. The problem was that he had to be careful about using explicitly religious imagery and iconography in order to do so. He had to come up with a new language. He had to come up with new symbols. Also, he was addressing a new kind of audience. His paintings would not be objects of prayer and adoration for a large congregation meeting together in a church. The era of church painting and commissions from Rome was over for painters like Hals. His paintings were going to be viewed by individuals. They were going to address single human beings who were, themselves, now engaged in a far more one-to-one relationship with their God, and their art.

For Hals, all the old rules were out the window. Nobody

had sufficiently established the new ones yet. I think you can even understand something about his loose style when you think of it that way. It is as if he was breaking things down, all the way to the level of the individual brushstroke, in order to build it all back up again. It isn't so much that he was painting without rules as that he was painting in search of new rules.

One of the paintings at the exhibit at The Met is often referred to by the title "Yonker Ramp and his Sweetheart" (1623). A young man in high spirits, clearly tipsy, is cavorting about with a lady of questionable repute. Anyway her face is red and flushed and she paws at the young fellow in immodest fashion. Let's think of her as a prostitute. Yonker Ramp is raising a toast to God-knows-what with one hand and cradling a dog's snout with his other hand. Is Yonker Ramp a contemporary version of the prodigal son? Are we being shown a scene in which the prodigal son is in the midst of wasting his money and reputation in dissolute living before his eventual return to an all-forgiving father? We can't be sure. Some scholars seem to think so, comparing the actions and poses in the painting with other works from the time.

One thing is certain: if the painting refers to the story of the prodigal son it does so without actually depicting the prodigal son. More intriguingly, it suggests that we don't need to depict the prodigal son of the Bible since we can go out and see the prodigal son right there in our local pub, down the street in Haarlem. And that matches up nicely with a bit of Protestant theology: namely, the idea that we do not need much mediation between ourselves and the truths of the Bible. The prohibition on the kind of religious painting that could be adored (the religious painting of the medieval church) practically forced painters like Hals into the everyday street scenes of his time. Rubens, a painter of the Counter Reformation, could, and did, work out the imagery of the Prodigal Son in direct depiction of the passages from Luke. Frans Hals had to work out similar themes as he was to find them in the actual experiences of contemporary 17th century Dutch life. Moreover, he was compelled, theologically speaking, to experiment in this direction. The Protestant teachings with which he was constantly surrounded admonished him to treat creation as he found it. "God," taught Martin Luther, "writes the gospel not in the Bible alone, but on trees and flowers and clouds and stars." Marrying that thought with the iconoclastic impulses of Dutch Protestantism led to an almost inexorable conclusion for Frans Hals: he would paint the stories, morals, and lessons of religion into the immediacy of the world as it was presenting itself right there in front of him.

The last thing we should probably note is the shock effect in many of Hals' paintings. The exhibition at The Met gives us, for instance, "Malle Babbe," Hals' portrait of a demented woman confined to a local workhouse. It is a disturbing painting of a disturbed woman made all the more disturbing by the knowledge that she actually existed and lived in the same workhouse as one of Hals' less-than-well sons. The shock effect of this painting is not, I think, to be taken as Hals' attempt to be lurid for the sake of it, or to shake up the mores of his contemporaries. That is a 20th century impulse. The shock effect within this work and other paintings by Hals--the leering faces, the intense expressions--is a reflection of the shock that Hals himself was experiencing. It is the theological shock of finding sin right there, redemption right there, blessedness and fallenness right there. It is a new language of painting made possible by the circumstances in which Frans Hals found himself: a Protestant man in a new theological landscape that needed, like all landscapes, someone to paint it.

Morgan Meis

Archive sketch New York City Draft Riots, 1863

Melville Redux

I can't get over the first two words of the poem: no sleep. No sleep. That's how Herman Melville began his poem, which is called "The House-top. A Night Piece." It was written in July of 1863. America was in the midst of the Civil War (the start of which is currently marking its 150th anniversary)—really in the thick of it.

In July of 1863 the action was in New York City. That's where the Draft Riots took place. For those who like to think of the story of the Civil War as roughly a story in which Right vanquishes Wrong, the Draft Riots are a troubling episode. The people of New York City, in 1863, were not happy with the Civil War and they didn't much want to fight in it. Many were particularly displeased by the Emancipation Proclamation, which Lincoln had announced earlier that year. A new round of the military draft was begun in July. Violence erupted quickly. And the violence was directed (also very quickly) at the free Black population of New York City. Black men and women who were captured by the marauding bands of rioters were beaten to death, tortured, set on fire. For a few days, the city descended into a nightmare. Melville describes it like this:

All civil charms
And priestly spells which late held hearts in awe—
Fear-bound, subjected to a better sway
Than sway of self; these like a dream dissolve,
And man rebounds whole æons back in nature.

Melville was always interested in the ways that man rebounds whole aeons back in nature. A biblical man and a fully contemporary man live simultaneously within the souls of the otherwise selfsame characters Melville created in his greatest literary works. "Call me Ishmael," says Ishmael at the beginning of Moby Dick. That opening line is so stark, so bold that it can hold its own against any literary work of the 20th or 21st century. There is nothing old fashioned about it. And yet, Ishmael wants his name to resonate back to the Old Testament, to the first son of Abraham about whom an angel of God proclaimed, "he shall be a wild ass of a man."

Melville performs the same trick of merging stark, proto-Modernist language with distinctly pre-modern ideas in his poem about the Draft Riots. "No sleep," he writes, and we are right there with him looking out over the rooftops of the buildings of New York City as the mobs set fires down in the streets below. It could be a Beat poem, or something written by a poet of today, up all night with insomnia on the Lower East Side. But then, look again at how Melville sees those rooftops and the modern city they represent.

Beneath the stars the roofy desert spreads
Vacant as Libya. All is hushed near by.
Yet fitfully from far breaks a mixed surf

Of muffled sound, the Atheist roar of riot.

We are back in the Old Testament again. New York City is but another landscape in the vicinity of Palestine, Assyria, Babylon. Later in the poem, Melville hears the rumble of the artillery coming into the city. Federal troops are going to clear the streets at gunpoint. The Town, Melville notes, is redeemed. And yet, a "grimy slur" remains. A stubborn fact refuses to go away. The claim of the Republic, the claim "that Man is naturally good" has been refuted once again in the events of the days that have just gone by. The New Man is the Old Man.

Melville included a footnote to his poem. "'I dare not write the horrible and inconceivable atrocities committed', says Froissart, in alluding to the remarkable sedition in France during his time. The like may be hinted of some proceedings of the draft-rioters." This fact, the human capacity to do what is horrible and inconceivable, was no surprise to Herman Melville, an Old Testament man through and through. Nevertheless, he couldn't sleep.

The House-Top. A Night Piece (July 1863)
Herman Melville

No sleep. The sultriness pervades the air
And blinds the brain--a dense oppression, such
As tawny tigers feel in matted shades,
Vexing their blood and making apt for ravage.
Beneath the stars the roofy desert spreads
Vacant as Libya. All is hushed near by.
Yet fitfully from far breaks a mixed surf
Of muffled sound, the Atheist roar of riot.

Yonder, where parching Sirius set in drought,
Balefully glares red Arson--there--and there.
The town is taken by its rats--ship-rats
And rats of the wharves. All civil charms
And priestly spells which late held hearts in awe--
Fear-bound, subjected to a better sway
Than sway of self; these like a dream dissolve
And man rebounds whole aeons back in nature.
Hail to the low dull rumble, dull and dead,
And ponderous drag that jars the wall.
Wise Draco comes, deep in the midnight roll
Of black artillery; he comes, though late;
In code corroborating Calvin's creed
And cynic tyrannies of honest kings;
He comes, nor parlies; and the Town, redeeemed,
Gives thanks devout; nor, being thankful, heeds
The grimy slur on the Republic's faith implied,
Which holds that man is naturally good,
And--more--is Nature's Roman, never to be scourged.

Morgan Meis

Still life by Giorgio Morandi

Giorgio Morandi

By the time Giorgio Morandi discovered himself as an artist he had reduced his universe to a handful of things. These were primarily bottles, tins, jugs, vases, and a few bowls. In a pinch, Morandi was perfectly happy with two tins and a vase. He would arrange the three things and then paint them. Generally he stuck to a muted palate: grays and beige, an overall preponderance of brown. Even when Morandi used brighter colors it still seemed like brown dressing up in drag for the occasion. His paintings do the opposite of pop. They simmer. They wait for you to come to them.

If Morandi painted his two tins and vase in one arrangement one day, he would move the vase a few inches and paint them anew the next day. These minute transformations amazed Morandi. He didn't need anything more. A slight change in the light, a subtle shift in direction, and his world of three things was forever fresh and new.

By all rights, these ought to be the most boring paintings in history. Nothing happens in them. They aren't quite abstract and so do not have the formal freedom to impress us with proportion and color like Mondrian or a wildness in pure movement and action like Pollock. They aren't full-bodied realism either and so cannot show us the richness of fruits and flowers and so forth from traditional still lives nor the striking still life deconstructions by someone like Cezanne. Morandi is content to do as close to nothing as a painter can do. He sits at his easel, year after year, shifts his two tins and the one damn vase, and then paints the scene in his own special vision of muted brownness.

Yet, these are extraordinarily beautiful and moving paintings. That's the shock of it. How did this homely and private Italian man pull it off? People who like to make a distinction between those who merely paint and those who are "painter's painters" like to brag about Morandi and his monkish dedication to the study of light and space and color. Well, he was monkish and unworldly and he loved nothing more than the act of painting, the physical process by which a human being applies a wet, colored substance to a canvass using strokes from a brush. People also like to point out that Morandi studied the paintings of Renaissance masters, particularly Piero della Francesca and Caravaggio. Morandi did learn from these painters, and he carried a certain Renaissance detachment to his studies of objects and the way that they look.

Being a painter's painter is fine, but it doesn't explain the broader appeal of Morandi's work. The results of these paintings are compelling beyond the lessons that they provide for those who think deeply about the practice of painting. The same is true of the Renaissance. It is possible to be excited by Morandi's canvasses without seeing them as continuing a tradition of the Quattro and Cinquecento.

Morandi himself never provided much of a roadmap. His most famous comment regarding his own work is, "nothing is more abstract than reality." It's a nicely gnomic utterance and interpreters have jumped all over it. Truly, late Morandi landscapes like Paesaggio (1962)—essentially a couple of blocks of white surrounded by fluffy gray-green spirals and a few hints of pink—are as close to abstraction as any realist painter would dare to get. When Morandi looked at a landscape he looked at it as areas of shape and color counterposed against other areas of shape and color.

But another famous Morandi quote reveals a rather straightforward naturalism. He said, "What interests me most is expressing what's in nature, in the visible world, that is." That's a commitment to representing the world as we actually encounter it. When you put these two things together you don't get a contradiction exactly, but you do get a certain amount of confusion. The two quotes lead us directly to a third: " Everything is a mystery, ourselves, and all things both simple and humble."

I think Morandi is exciting because he is sneaky and he's a liar. He pretends that he's just a modest man letting objects be objects and letting nature be nature. His pastels and repertoire of browns dull the senses, draw you in to his Circean web. Once you're drawn in, Morandi has you. He takes you through a nearly infinite set of examples of how much control he has over the very objects that normally mark our limits as human beings. Every day we are impinged upon. Every day we serve the mute indifference of things, stuff that we cannot control.

Morandi pared his universe down to just a few of those things. He took away the background and the foreground. He shifted everything into a color spectrum of his own choosing. You can actually watch him do it. In the still lives from the late 30's, there's still a sense of menace in some of the objects. An uncomfortable contrast in white and black and red makes the vases and bottles project outright menace. Natura morta (1937, V. 221) and natura morta (1938, V. 225) are chaotic and threatening works; the objects are not under any direct artistic control. By the early 40s, Morandi has figured things out, literally. He has decided how he wants things to be. Things, objects, are going to play by his rules.

Thus the obsessiveness of Morandi's last two decades. He knew what he was up against and he knew what he had to do. He had to make objects conform to his vision while still portraying them as real objects. So, he arranged his bottles and tins and vases in one way and then he arranged them in another. He painted them in the morning and the evening and at night. He observed them through shifts of light and color and position. For twenty-five years, Morandi painted canvass after canvass using the same handful of tins and bottles and vases, sometimes shifting their position no more than an inch or two. Always, he was able to overcome these variables and make the objects look as he wanted them to look. Take a painting like natura morta (1954, V. 906). This is a vase and three tins not as they are found on an actual kitchen table, but as Morandi would have them. It is soothing and rapturous to stare at that painting, to know it exists, to realize that one man was so able to master the world immediately before him—calmly, surely, on his own terms and none other.

So, in a sense, Morandi was another great egotist of 20th century art. The modest scale and subject matter of his paintings tricks us into talking about Morandi as a painter of humility and small gestures. But that is wrong. He chose his own field of battle—the kitchen table and a handful of objects upon it—and he waged a war on all those material things that resist our attempts to understand them. We may never understand them, say Morandi's paintings, but we can make of them something grand, something brown, and something completely our own.

Paterson, New Jersey

Paterson, New Jersey

I like to take the train from Penn Station out to Paterson. It stops in Secaucus Junction, a new and gleaming place that never seems to have anyone in it, just cavernous halls of light marble and a lonely bar tucked in one corner, the woodwork of which seems laughable and out of place and therefore sympathetic. The barkeep told me it would be a great place to work if a few hundred more costumers came through every day.

I always ride in the space between train cars from Penn to Secaucus. It is loud and feels like what I imagine train travel to have been like in the olden days; jarring, big, transformative. The train smells more like itself between the cars, especially when it is raining in the evening. As you bumble your way out of the big city and into the tunnels under the Hudson you can watch the rivulets of water splashing down into the lonely puddles that pockmark the railway trenches of the far West Side. The last few streams of light make their way through the clouds and glimmer in the raindrops and the dirt like a faded painting.

I don't object to the changes in all things. I don't object to the fact that all experiences are washed away in time.

But I like the way that the little metal platform between train cars is protecting a feeling that has barely changed for generations.

The train pulls out of Secaucus Junction and then putters along through the marshy fields that make up the Jersey wilds just outside of Manhattan. There is tantalizingly little to see until the industrial ruins of Paterson begin to show themselves with not much fanfare. The train ride doesn't get somewhere so much as end.

***

No one knows exactly why William Carlos Williams chose Paterson as the subject and location for a new poetry. He was working on his variable triadic foot. It was a new meter, so he said. It has never been entirely clear how it's supposed to scan. Maybe Williams himself never really understood it. But he was messing around, trying to capture the American idiom and thereby the American experience. He stayed in New Jersey while all the other Americans went to Paris or wherever chasing something they thought was going to turn out big. For some it did. For some it didn't. Williams stayed and stayed some more. He wasn't having fun, he was working. He was listening to the Paterson Falls and he was crafting in his forge. "No ideas but in things": a new poetic empiricism.

***

These days Paterson is broken, let's be honest. She has her honor, like an old hooker, but she's broken. It is probably impossible to know what finally breaks a city, what makes it give up and fall apart into petty fiefdoms and the inability to live. All the factors, of course, play their roles: economics, politics, the ongoing terrible American abyss of race. But something else happens when a city breaks, something nobody has a handle on exactly. In that way a city can be like a person. And no one can say precisely what happens to a person when they walk outside and look at the bricks around them, the houses and buildings, and suddenly see nothing at all. What seemed to be a world of meaning around them, the context for living a life, turns into something empty and irrelevant. When that happens you're not living in the world anymore, you're simply existing alongside it.

***

There's a statue of Alexander Hamilton standing at the Paterson Falls, just looking. The Paterson Falls ought to be a marvel of the East Coast. They are nature in its aspect of the sublime. To one's consistent amazement, they sit there in the midst of a neighborhood, right there in the lap of a city that suddenly shifts gears and gives way to a torrent of rushing water and black rocks.

Hamilton stands there and watches the falls decade after decade. Not many people remember it anymore but a battle took place here long ago. It was a struggle between competing dreams. To simplify, one was Jeffersonian and one was Hamiltonian. Jefferson dreamed of something agrarian, something manageable. He wanted a small democracy built up of autonomous men. It was a decent dream so far as it went. Hamilton dreamed of something else, of the wheels of industry churning out goods and wealth within an urban milieu that the world hadn't seen yet.

One wonders what Hamilton would have thought about the actual history of Paterson. The way that Paterson ended up being intertwined with the American imagination, the American tragicomedy, the American story, is hundreds of times more complicated than he could have dreamed. But he dreamed it all up nonetheless. Now he stands at the Falls with his back to the city and watches, just looking.

Morgan Meis

David Foster Wallaca, section of photo
© Giovanni Giovannetti / Effigie

The Pale King

David Foster Wallace's final book is boring. On that, everyone seems to agree. We understand, too, that Wallace intended it to be boring. David Foster Wallace, in the years before he killed himself in 2008, was writing, after all, a long novel about the IRS. He hadn't finished the book when he died. So, we are left with the incomplete remnants of what he was still in the process of creating. But it is easy to see, in reading The Pale King, published from all the material that DFW was working on before his death, that he fully intended to write a book that would produce long stretches of boredom for the reader. He wanted to produce boredom, he wanted to reflect on boredom, and he wanted, finally, to love boredom.

The most important piece of writing to come out about David Foster Wallace in some time was written by Maria Bustillos for The Awl in early April of this year. Maria is an unabashed fan of David Foster Wallace and wrote a book (Dorkismo: the Macho of the Dork) that includes the chapter, "David Foster Wallace: the Dork Lord of American Letters." Being both a writer and a fan, Bustillos wanted to know. After the suicide, she wanted to know. She wanted what many of us who admired the writer wanted: more of the man. She hoped, as we all hoped, that secrets would be revealed and that the secrets of the interior David Foster Wallace might also shed some light on his terrible, impressive, and depressing final act, the taking of his own life.

Maria Bustillos decided to go to the source in the attempt to find out what DFW was thinking. She had the strength to go to his papers and to read them. The papers exist. His books exist too, the books from DFW's private library, many of which are heavily annotated. There are notes and jottings and lists and letters. It can all be found at the Ransom Center at the University of Texas at Austin. Maria Bustillos went there and she started to read, she started to look through all that material. What she found surprised her. Days after being there she was still trying, as she put it, "to cram my eyeballs all the way back in where they belong." One thing that surprised Bustillos was:

> ...the number of popular self-help books in the collection, and the care and attention with which he read and reread them. I mean stuff of the best-sellingest, Oprah-level cheesiness and la-la reputation was to be found in Wallace's library. Along with all the Wittgenstein, Husserl and Borges, he read John Bradshaw, Willard Beecher, Neil Fiore, Andrew Weil, M. Scott Peck and Alice Miller. Carefully.

David Foster Wallace was reading this self-help material because he was trying to put himself back together after having nearly lost himself. He almost died, to put it simply. He was addicted to drugs and alcohol and he was killing himself. He went into treatment. He attended rehab and AA meetings and became involved with Twelve Step programs. In doing so, he came to realize that his striving for genius, his need to produce works of genius and to prove to the world that he was a genius was part of the problem. Those feelings, those impulses were taking him out of the world, making him feel isolated and alone, cutting him off from the experiences of his fellow man. He became interested in killing the genius and becoming, once again, a human being. For him, the self-help books of John Bradshaw were more helpful in doing this than the philosophical works of Husserl. That's how DFW saw it, at least.

The Pale King must be looked at, then, within the context of the ongoing process in which David Foster Wallace was trying to bring himself down to size. The character named David Wallace in The Pale King is a caseworker for the IRS. He is an anonymous toiler in a giant bureaucracy. Not just any bureaucracy. The IRS. Is there a less prestigious, less desirable job in all the world? There are chapters in The Pale King that discuss arcane matters of tax law down to the tiniest detail. There are painstaking discussions of the appearance, history, and significance of an IRS office building in Peoria, Illinois. There are descriptions of the daily goings-on at the IRS office that read like the following:

Howard Cardwell shifts slightly in his chair and turns a page. Lane Dean Jr. traces his jaw's outline with his ring finger. Ed Shackleford turns a page. Elpidia Carter turns a page. Ken Wax attaches a Memo to a file. Anand Singh turns a page. Jay Landauer and Ann Williams turn a page almost precisely in sync although they are in different rows and cannot see each other.

David Foster Wallace seems like he is trying to melt into the boredom of these passages. In fact, that is exactly what he is doing. The sentence that comes directly after the passage just quoted above reads, "Boris Katz bobs with a slight Hasidic motion as he crosschecks a page with a collection of figures." Suddenly, the boredom is leading to something more profound, an attitude of reverence even. DFW is not simply trying to punish us, or himself, with the tiresome monotony of life at the IRS. "It turns out that bliss," Wallace wrote in his notes for the novel, "a second-by-second joy + gratitude at the gift of being alive, conscious—lies on the other side of crushing, crushing boredom."

There is a two-step process here. First, you accept the mundane. You accept the boredom and the toil of life in general. You even willingly push it to its extreme and sign up, for instance, to work at the IRS for the rest of your life. There you can become one with the boredom. You can have an experience that is not, on the face of it, special in any single way. But if you are truly attentive to the details, if you concentrate on the minutia like a Hasid davening before a sacred text, then you have come out through the other side of boredom into a heightened relationship to the here and now.

In fact, the collection of characters at the IRS that Wallace tracks in The Pale King are all mystics of the boring in one way or another. One character with almost autistic literalness and attention to the details of tax-code reaches states of concentration that find him levitating above his desk. Another character spent his childhood in the obsessive, body-contorting, yogi-like process of attempting to kiss every spot of flesh on his own body. These people have come to the IRS not because they've given up on life, but because they have discovered what they consider to be a secret at the heart of life. It is the boring that leads you to real reality. It is the mundane that is the door into the extraordinary. The things that seem, at first, to be exciting and pleasurable are actually a trap. They lead to emptiness.

That is, in fact, an idea that David Foster Wallace had already explored in the book that made him famous. Infinite Jest is, among other things, a novel about the emptiness of contemporary life. All the entertainment, all the distraction leads to naught. It is the road of despair. You have to find something else, you have to find a way out of it. Infinite Jest is about zeroing in on that problem. The Pale King is DFW's attempt to make the next step into a possible solution. If you can exist and thrive within the IRS, if you can love the IRS, if you can become one with the IRS, then you can do anything, you can be OK with any aspect of the world as it is given to us, any aspect of mass society from its empty entertainment to its mindless bureaucracy. There is a passage where the sometimes narrator of the novel, the fictional David Wallace explains this quite clearly:

> I'm not the smartest person, but even during that whole pathetic, directionless period, I think that deep down I knew that there was more to my life and to myself than just the ordinary psychological impulses for pleasure and vanity that I let drive me. That there were depths to me that were not bullshit or childish but profound, and were not abstract but actually much realer than my clothes or my self image, and that blazed in an almost sacred way—I'm being serious; I'm not just trying to make it sound more dramatic than it was—and that these realest, most profound parts of me involved not drives or appetites but simple attention, awareness, if only I could stay awake off speed.

It doesn't really matter how autobiographical that passage actually is (though I suspect it is very much so). The logic of moving from the psychological impulses for pleasure and vanity to the sacred depths of the self was real to David Foster Wallace and translates directly into the fictional experience of David Wallace, employee of the IRS in Peoria, Illinois. "Simple attention, awareness" is a powerful force in The Pale King. In the novel, DFW has turned the entire bureaucracy of the IRS into a secret hiding place for those who seek to perfect the art of paying attention.

You could say that David Foster Wallace was looking for a place for prayer in modern American life. It was Simone Weil, the great Catholic/Jewish philosopher and mystic of the 20th century, who once said that, "Absolutely unmixed attention is prayer." That is exactly the power all the characters of The Pale King are learning about, absolute unmixed attention. The IRS building in Peoria, as Wallace imagines it, is practically a monastery. The acolytes are at their examiners tables learning how to pray. The US Tax Code becomes the new catechism.

Looking at it this way, you could also call The Pale King David Foster Wallace's version of an 11th Step. According to the literature of AA, the 11th Step is where members of AA "Sought through prayer and meditation to improve our conscious contact with God as we understood Him, praying only for knowledge of His will for us and the power to carry that out." The earlier steps in the Twelve Step tradition are largely about clearing away the bondage of self, learning to reintegrate oneself into the "stream of life." The 11th Step is about formalizing that process into a daily practice. It is, in DFW's language, about creating habits for simple attention, awareness. It is about finding ways to worship. Here's how Wallace put it in his now-famous 2005 commencement address at Kenyon College:

Because here's something else that's weird but true: in the day-to day trenches of adult life, there is actually no such thing as atheism. There is no such thing as not worshipping. Everybody worships. The only choice we get is what to worship. And the compelling reason for maybe choosing some sort of god or spiritual-type thing to worship -- be it JC or Allah, bet it YHWH or the Wiccan Mother Goddess, or the Four Noble Truths, or some inviolable set of ethical principles -- is that pretty much anything else you worship will eat you alive. If you worship money and things, if they are where you tap real meaning in life, then you will never have enough, never feel you have enough. It's the truth. Worship your body and beauty and sexual allure and you will always feel ugly. And when time and age start showing, you will die a million deaths before they finally grieve you. On one level, we all know this stuff already. It's been codified as myths, proverbs, clichés, epigrams, parables; the skeleton of every great story. The whole trick is keeping the truth up front in daily consciousness.

The Pale King is a novelistic exercise in and exploration of that trick, the trick of keeping the truth up front in daily consciousness. Why did he kill himself then? The text of The Pale King, as we have it, suggests that he was getting somewhere. He was doing his own version of the 11th Step. He was getting better. He was even, maybe, continuing to show the rest of us ways forward through the most difficult problems and questions anyone can confront. He was facing the emptiness of modern life head on and taking it seriously. He actually thought that a person can ask real questions like "How am I to live?" and come up with real answers. And then he killed himself and the whole thing collapses. Is DFW's 11th Step thus a false solution? Are his ideas about what it means to have absolute unmixed attention a route to despair and finally to suicide?

I doubt there are any truly satisfying answers to that question. DFW's suicide, especially in the light of what he was trying to do in The Pale King, is troubling all the way down to its core. It is terrifying because it suggests that the possibility of absolute despair never goes away. Simone Weil seems to have gone in that direction too, starving herself to death in solidarity with her fellow French countryman suffering during WWII. Or maybe, (it is sometimes suggested) she was trying to emulate the suffering and despair of Christ. At its heart, her death, like the death of David Foster Wallace is a mystery and a painful conundrum. Perhaps it is simply the case that if you've been convinced that life can have real meaning, that there is an absolute good with which we can have contact, it must also be conceded that there is an absolute bad. And when you have opened yourself to the absolute good you have also, potentially, exposed yourself to the absolute bad. Lurking behind DFW's critique of contemporary culture and its celebration of entertainment and distraction is the darker thought that equates our drive for pleasure with evil. He is touching on the territory of original sin and the possibility of redemption. The most radical thing David Foster Wallace may have achieved was to raise the matter once again of good and evil in the post-modern world in which nothing is supposed to matter very much. If he was right about that, if he was on the right track, then he was telling us about the most important things there are. He was telling us about life and death issues or issues, maybe, even more important than that. Was he trying to tell us about our souls? Who knows? Surely, though, he was trying to tell us the truth. He was trying to speak the truth and, ultimately, he died for it.

Morgan Meis

Archive photo Katyn Massacre

Katyn

On the morning of April 10th, 2010, a ball of flame erupted in the forest outside of Smolensk, Russia. A plane had crashed. Everyone on board was killed. This was a significant fact, especially for Poland. The President of Poland was on that plane, along with a significant portion of his Cabinet. Ryszard Kaczorowski, the last President of Poland in exile, was aboard the plane. He was the man who passed the presidential insignia to Lech Walesa as the first democratically elected President of Poland since WWII. The chiefs of staff of the Polish Army, Navy, and Air Force were aboard the plane. The deputy foreign minister was aboard the plane, as well as the head of the National Bank and the head of the National Security Bureau. Important lawmakers and members of parliament were aboard that plane, as well as top military leaders, bishops, priests, political advisors, and aides. Ninety-six people died.

It was an incredible event, for a country to lose so many of its top civilian and military leaders in a single blow like that. But that doesn't even begin to tell the full story. These people were Polish after all, and in Poland, tragedies have a way of magnifying and expanding through history. That so many important Poles would die in the forests outside of Smolensk was almost unbelievable in its significance. The rest of the world was less aware of the background history and thus less aware of how strange an event that plane crash really was. You see, this was not the first time that the forests around Smolensk had claimed the lives of so many prominent Poles. It had all happened before. In shocking and unexpected ways, history was repeating itself.

We must go back to the early days of WWII now. Vyachslav Molotov, the foreign minister of what was then the Soviet Union, and Joachim von Ribbentrop, the German foreign minister under Adolf Hitler, had agreed to a pact whereby the Soviets and the Nazis would split Europe and agree not to fight one another. This is the infamous Treaty of Non-Aggression signed in 1939. It was a pact doomed to be broken, a task Hitler took care of two years later when he launched a surprise attack on the Soviets only to meet his own doom at Stalingrad in 1943, a battle that, for all practical purposes, meant the end of the Third Reich. But before all that, before the Nazi war machine had turned toward Western Europe in all its fury, the Nazis and the Soviets were busy invading Poland together. Much of Eastern Poland was quickly swallowed up by the Soviets, the Nazis taking the rest.

As the Red Army moved across Poland the NKVD, precursor to what later became the KGB, was busy rounding up Polish army officials and other professionals—university professors, politicians, public intellectuals, scientists—and putting them into concentration camps. It was unclear what was to be done with them. Then, finally, the secret order came down on the 5th of March, 1940. Stalin and other top Soviet leaders had decided what to do. These people, more than 22,000 of them, all told, were to be executed, in secret, and dumped into mass graves.

The forests around Smolensk became a killing ground of vast proportions. Other sights were chosen closer to Moscow and near a number of labor camps that made up Stalin's Gulag system. Outside of Smolensk, the killing was done in the Katyn forest. More than 4,400 Poles were shot and buried there in mass graves, many of them among the most important military and civilian leaders. Vasili Blokhin was even brought in to handle some of the killing at the Osthashkov camp. Blokhin, a Major-General, was head executioner for the NKVD and a favorite of Stalin. It is estimated that he personally shot and killed 7,000 people, one by one, during the Katyn massacres. The Guinness Book of World Records, in fact, named him the world's "Most Prolific Executioner" in 2010.

High-level officers had their arms tied behind their backs and were bustled down into a basement after signing papers. Pushed into a small room by guards, the prisoner was forced to his knees while another man would step out from behind the door, put a pistol to the back of the prisoner's head, and pull the trigger. The body would be pulled out a second door or through a hatch at the top of the room. The room was quickly swabbed down for the next execution. Out in the forest the procedure was roughly the same. Groups of Poles were loaded onto lorries, the infamous Black Marias, and driven out to pits dug by Soviet tractors. Prisoners were hustled quickly from the lorries and then bound at the wrist. Pushed over to the edge of the pit, a Soviet agent would step in from the side and place his revolver to the skull of the victim and quickly pull the trigger. The dead body would slump down into the mass grave with the hundreds of other bodies already there. Before any of these people could register what was happening to them, they were dead.

For this job, the NKVD liked to use the German 7.65 mm Walther PPK pistol. This had a twofold purpose. First, those pistols tended to be pretty reliable. They rarely misfired and they had the ability to deliver a kill shot almost every time. Vasili Blokhin liked to use the Walther PPK because it kicked back less and therefore did less damage to his wrist after thousands upon thousands of firings. Using a German pistol was also useful for the fact that the bodies, if ever discovered, might look like they were killed by the Nazis instead of the Soviets. As it turned out, the corpses were discovered just a year later in the summer of 1941 when the Nazis had turned against the Soviets and were on the march east, taking all the ground that had so recently been captured by the Soviets. The Nazis, seeing an opportunity for some easy propaganda against the Soviets, released pictures and information about the massacre to the world press. It was proclaimed a Soviet atrocity against the Poles. The Soviets protested, blaming the Nazis for the killings. The din of ongoing war muffled the details of the debate. A year later, the Wehrmacht was stopped at Stalingrad and the tide of battle swung, once more, the other direction. The Soviets re-took the ground they had lost and marched all the way to Berlin. Smolensk was Soviet again. But not just Smolensk—Poland too had fallen within the Soviet orbit and would remain there until the final collapse of the Soviet Union in the early 1990s.

With Smolensk in Soviet hands, with Poland fully in the Soviet Bloc and occupied by Soviet troops, the Katyn massacre was now, "officially" designated a Nazi atrocity. More often than not, Poles were encouraged not to speak of it at all. But they did speak of it. The memory of Katyn became an important symbol and rallying cry. To speak of Katyn, to remember Katyn, was a way to hold truth up in the face of all the lies. Postwar Poland was, after all, a place awash in lies. The fundamental lie was that Poland had ever wanted to be a part of the Soviet sphere of influence and Warsaw Pact in the first place. In fact, Poland had been forced against her will. Poland had been beaten into submission. The name of that submission, the name of the humiliation, would be Katyn.

***

For almost fifty years, Poles had to live with the official lie that the Katyn massacres had not been perpetrated by the Soviets and that the People's Republic of Poland (the name of the Polish state during the years of Soviet occupation), was their own idea and not something imposed upon them from Moscow. All that changed in 1990. The Berlin Wall came down, the Soviet Union dissolved, everything transformed all at once.

That same year, Mikhail Gorbachev admitted that the victims of the Katyn massacres had been executed by the NKVD. On the 13th of April, 1990, the Soviet Union officially expressed its apology for the Katyn massacres and declared April 13th Katyn Memorial Day. Boris Yeltsin later released classified documents about the massacre and a steady stream of documents has been released since then, including Stalin's signed memo authorizing the executions.

By the late 1990s, talk of a memorial to the Katyn massacres had begun in earnest. Yeltsin and then Polish president Aleksander Kwasnieski agreed to initiate the process of building a memorial that would commemorate both the victims of the Katyn massacre and the victims of the two other NKVD execution sites for internal Russian prisoners nearby. In the summer of 2000, the Katyn National Memorial Complex was opened just outside of Smolensk, built with the cooperation of the Ministry of Culture of the Russian Federation and a consortium of Polish groups known as the Council of Preserving Memory, Struggle and Martyrdom.

This was the final step, it seemed, in the long process of historical recognition for the original crime. This was the moment of reconciliation. This was the moment when old wounds could finally begin to heal. That, after all, is what memorials are for.

***

In fact, there is a paradox at the heart of every memorial. We set up memorials in order to remember. Memorial, as the word suggests, is about memory. The memorial is thus a physical manifestation of memory. It makes memory a real thing in the world. Where there is a memorial, presumably, there is a permanent memory. Maybe the simplest, oldest and most iconic form of the memorial is the stone marker. Stone is strong and real. Stone lasts longer than flesh every time. And so we attempt to put memories into stone, hard permanent stone.

But here is where the paradox comes in. We put up memorials to remember, but we also put them up to forget. Making a memorial is partly about putting history away, putting tragedy (or triumph) into stone and then moving on. Memory held too close is dangerous to life. You cannot spend all your time remembering or else nothing new happens. The past can be an abyss. No one wants to fall into the abyss. And so we do something to mark the moment. We put up a memorial to the trauma, to the important event, to the struggle, to whatever. Putting up the memorial is an act of payment. It is a payment to the past in order to proceed into the future. Simply moving on would be too painful. It would feel as if the proper payment had not been made. We need to make the payment or else we pay for the failure to do so in the wages of guilt. To pay our dues, to assuage the guilt, to move forward with the sense that the past has been given its respect, we put up a monument. The monument says that we can start forgetting now, to let the past be the past.

We see this aspect of forgetting in all memorials. One of the obvious but not always mentioned aspects of Maya Lin's memorial for the Vietnam War is how funereal the thing is. The slabs of black stone with the names and dates are like a giant tombstone sweeping sideways across the green grass. It is a tombstone to the American individuals who died in the Vietnam War, but it is also a tombstone to the war itself. It says, "we can let the thing die now, we can let it go." The people are dead, and the war is dead too. It was important to do that in 1982, when the Memorial was officially dedicated, because the Vietnam War was threatening to remain in the present longer than its due. It wouldn't go to rest. Maya Lin figured out a way to initiate that process, to begin, slowly but steadily, to forget. It worked, and the memorial was a triumph even after much early controversy, because people were ready. In their hearts they were ready. And something changed about the

Vietnam War after Lin's memorial went up. The war began to give up its hold on the present and go away into the past. The Lin Memorial initiated the process of real forgetting. Every year now, every passing day, the Vietnam War is forgotten. It is painful to put it this way, it sounds wrong. But it isn't wrong. Some forgetting needs to happen if only because new tragedies, new triumphs, new traumas come along and need their space.

***

The memorial to the Katyn massacre in the woods just outside of Smolensk in the western part of Russia not too far from the border with Belarus, is a beautiful memorial. This is largely due to the forest in which the memorial is located, a natural setting that the makers of the memorial did much to respect and utilize. In this forest, the trees are particularly stately. They just grow that way. There are pines and birch trees mostly. The forest is neither too dense nor too sparse. The trees grow at a respectful distance from one another and straight up into the sky. This gives a feeling of openness at eye level. You can really see where you are in the forest of Katyn, you can get your bearings. The forest floor is lightly covered with ferns and mosses. And then the tree trunks draw the eye up, always up. As you look upward, the trees begin to form a canopy. The branches lift out and over the space of the forest. There is a cathedral effect--there is no other way to describe it. Through the leafy openings of this forest cathedral can be glimpsed the blue sky. And you can't help thinking, the people who were dragged out and shot here glimpsed this for a moment. They saw the forest cathedral and the sky before they dropped down into those pits.

The pits are there too. A circle of sorts has been dug around the area where the killings took place. This creates an internal wall. Along the wall are metal boxes that each bear the names and dates of the individuals killed there. Above this wall of boxes is a layer of earth, which creates the effect of looking beneath the earth, seeing into the pits that were originally dug to be mass graves, nameless graves. Now, the names have been restored beneath the earth. The pit has been given back to human history as a small triumph over the forces that would have cancelled these names, these individuals, forever. The forest, the pit, the names. Those three elements form the essence of the Katyn Memorial in the forest outside of Smolensk.

There is an air of solidity and permanence to the memorial, something that says this will be here for a very long time. It has persistence. At the same time, it is a place that says we can put the past away. As you walk from the road toward the memorial, a giant red geometrical archway splits the path into three routes. You can go to the right directly toward the place where the Poles were killed, or you can go to the left, toward the graves for thousands of Russian citizens who were also killed here over the years, during the time of Stalin's terror, during the Great Purges. And you can go a middle way that is unnamed, unclaimed. From the middle, a person can wander freely across death without its national distinctions.

Memory and forgetting, they both have a role to play in the memorial at Katyn. Still, there is a tension. It can be felt as you walk through the trees and make your way from one path to the other. The path to the right is marked by a Polish flag, the path to the left is marked by a Russian flag. The

Poles who were killed at Katyn were killed by Russians, the same Russians who had made a pact with the Nazis to rip Poland apart and share the pieces. But since Smolensk is in Russia, this cannot be a site simply of Polish national tragedy and Polish nationalism. It has to be a shared site; it has to be a site that moves past the blame, that forgoes condemnation. So, an uneasiness lingers here. The memorial cannot overcome that tension completely. By existing at all, the memorial is drawing attention to the crime, bringing it back into the present. The memorial is struggling to do two things at once, to do justice to memory, making the memories alive for the present, and to tame those memories, to put them back away again where they can rest. But every time you bring memories out of the past, they threaten to become real again. Every decision around the making of the Katyn memorial, every debate about exactly who would get memorialized there and under what context, brought out the old rivalries and the old mistrust. Maybe that is what can be felt in the forest of Katyn, the carefulness. Every gesture, every stone, every twist in every path had to be decided upon with the utmost of care or the whole project would have fallen apart. The Russians might have gotten mad, the Poles might have gotten mad. The delicate balance between remembering and forgetting sits on a razor's edge at Katyn.

The Katyn Memorial most successfully overcomes the dangers of remembering by focusing on the actual individuals who died. The individuals, the memorial is saying, are the most important now. The specific political and historical context in which they died is of less significance. So, we can forget a little. Specifically, we can forget a little bit about blame and causality and victimhood. Here, the memorial seems to say, are Russians and Poles who were brought here against their will to be murdered in a time when death ran rampant beyond anyone's control. Let that be the final word on the matter. In the name of moving forward, in the name of leaving some things of the past back in the past, let that be the last word. People died here, wrongly, and we mourn them.

***

There was a memorial ceremony held at Katyn only a few days before the tragic plane crash in the late Spring of 2011. The memorial service was attended by both Russians and Poles. Vladimir Putin was there, as was Donald Tusk, the Prime Minister of Poland. They spoke of remembering but also of forgetting, forgetting past grievances, letting the pain subside. Putin made a speech at the memorial service, saying, "No matter how difficult it is, we must move toward each other, remembering everything but understanding that we can't live only in the past."

But it was this very fact, the forgetting and moving on part of the memorial ceremony, that didn't sit right with a number of Poles. It didn't sit right with the President of Poland, Lech Kaczynski, who was not invited to the ceremony by the Russians and was never known as the most accommodating of fellows. It didn't sit right with a number of other politicians, nor with a number of generals and military officers. They did not feel ready to do that kind of forgetting. They wanted to keep some aspect of the pain alive, to keep it present. And there is something understandable in this too. These Poles wanted recognition not just for the tragedy itself but for the long history of lies about the tragedy. They wanted recognition for the long history of lack of recognition. That can be the most difficult kind of recognition to get.

So, Lech Kaczynski decided that he would conduct his own ceremony. That's why he chartered the plane, that's why he filled it up with all the other high-level Poles who felt the way he did. That's why they set off to the Smolensk airport on the foggy morning of April 10th, 2010. By the time the plane arrived in Smolensk airspace the fog had gotten very thick. The air control tower in Smolensk told them it wasn't safe to land, that they should go to Minsk instead. Kaczynski and, presumably, other people on the plane didn't see it that way. There was, reportedly, a great deal of tension in the cockpit between the pilots, who understood the very real dangers of landing in those conditions, and the VIPs who wanted to get to the Katyn Memorial at any cost. They ordered the pilot to land. The plane made a pass over the airport and then turned around to attempt a landing. As it came in lower, the plane shook and was buffeted by the choppy air. The pilots began to lose control. The plane struck the tops of some of the trees, the tall trees of the forests around Smolensk. The plane began to come apart in the air. Some part of the plane struck the ground. The fuselage disintegrated and the human bodies within were flung down to the forest floor beneath as pieces of the aircraft crashed and burned along with them. In seconds, everyone was dead.

And now, there is another memorial to be found in the forests around Smolensk. Another group of Polish luminaries from the realm of politics and the military has been claimed. Right now, the memorial to the plane crash consists mostly of crosses and a large stone brought to the site near one of the landing fields of the Smolensk airport as a marker. There are pictures and candles and personal memorabilia placed near the crosses and near the stone. This new memorial is raw, marked by the impromptu gestures of the recently grieving. String outlines can still be found (in the summer of 2011) in the fields nearby, marking the spots where specific bodies were found in the hours after the crash.

***

This makeshift memorial to the plane crash is now like a supplement to the main memorial at Katyn. It is a supplement not just because of the circumstances of the plane crash, the fact that Lech Kaczynski and his colleagues were on their way to the Katyn memorial, but because the plane crash happened as a direct result of the same tensions that linger at the Katyn memorial and linger, in some form or other, at all memorials. Remembering is dangerous. Memorials have a dark side. The pain that memorials memorialize constantly threatens to erupt again into the present.

In some ways, Lech Kaczynski didn't want to forget and he didn't want to move on. Part of him did recognize the need to move on, of course. In the speech he was to give at the memorial he was going to make a gesture toward further reconciliation between Russia and Poland. He was going to make a call for further healing of the wounds. But there were aspects of Katyn that were very difficult for Kaczynski to let go of for the simple reason that his own identity was wrapped up in them. He called the cover-up of Katyn the "foundational fraud of the Polish People's Republic." The flip side of this claim is that the acknowledgment of Katyn is then the foundational truth for an authentic Poland. That idea, the idea of Katyn as the truth of Poland, was something that Kaczynski wanted to keep alive. He wanted the historical memory of Katyn to live in the present. He wanted it to live in the present because he wanted it to guide peoples' actions now. One of Lech Kaczynski's pet projects was an antiballistic missile defense system that was to be provided by the Americans and directed against the Russians. This was a source of great displeasure to the Russians and surely one of the reasons why Kaczyniski and his people were not invited to the Katyn Memorial ceremony attended by Putin.

There is a certain Polish mindset, understandable from the perspective of history, that says Poland will always define itself in opposition to Russia. It goes back to WWII, but it goes back before that. It goes to the Polish-Soviet War that broke out just after WWI and led to the establishment of the first Polish nation state, the Second Republic. And it goes back further. It goes back to the Partitions of the late 18th century when Poland ceased to be Poland and was carved up between the powers of Russia, Prussia, and Hapsburg Austria. It goes back before that, too, to the Polish–Muscovite War of the early 17th century when the Poles marched all the way to Moscow and then, in later years, were pushed back in a series of defeats in which the city of Smolensk, not incidentally, passed back and forth between Polish and Russian hands. All these past wars, these struggles of guns and politics, were on Stalin's mind too the day he signed the papers for the mass executions at Katyn. He was striking a preemptive blow against any independent Poland that might emerge from the ashes of WWII and then rise to be another thorn in Russia's side.

He was trying to lop Poland off at the head, to kill its leadership and to leave Poland rudderless and adrift in the postwar scenario to come.

And all of these thoughts must have been in the mind of Lech Kaczynski when he got word from the Russian control tower at the Smolensk airport that the plane couldn't land. Thousands of voices must have been screaming in his head at that moment. The old voices of Katyn were telling him that he must land no matter what. So he decided to land. And that landing became, itself, another Katyn, another case in which Russia—this time unintentionally and through no fault of its own—had lopped off the head of Poland. It is impossible, I think, to imagine the decision to go ahead and land that plane with all the dangers involved unless you can hear those voices, unless you can feel the tremendous weight of history that was coming to bear on the individuals inside that plane. They felt directly responsible for the memory of Katyn, a memory that, for them, breathed life into an entire nation, making it what it is. They had to land that plane.

It is terrible to contemplate this fact, but the immediate result of the plane crash was to realize Kaczynski's purpose and to make the memory of Katyn very alive indeed. The tragedy of the past was carried forward into the events of the present, just like Lech Kaczynski always wanted. His tragic death, and the deaths of the other ninety-five people on board, virtually assured that people in Poland and around the world were going to be talking about Katyn and thinking about Katyn. The memorial ceremony three days before attended by Donald Tusk and Vladimir Putin was having the opposite effect. It was pushing the memory of Katyn further into the past. Tusk and Putin had actually shaken hands while standing over the graves of Katyn. Tusk remarked in his speech at the event that the dead of Katyn would have wanted to see reconciliation between Poland and Russia. The voices of Katyn's past were being evoked in order to put the historical event to rest, to begin to cover it over with forgetting.

The plane crash immediately reversed this process. It made the original tragedy of Katyn raw again, in an instant. Accusations about who was at fault immediately began to be tossed around. The conspiracy theories (baseless as they were) that immediately cropped up about Russian involvement and complicity in the crash served to freshen up that old theme of Polish tragedy and Russian perfidy. In his death, Lech Kaczynski had managed to create a supplementary memorial to the original Katyn memorial that would serve to halt the process of forgetting initiated at the original site. Nobody was going to forget this anytime soon. Lech Kaczynski had discovered, despite himself and without intending to, a way to keep history from fading away into the past. It cost many human lives to do so. But the surest way to make an old tragedy new again is to repeat it. It is almost as if history was ready to provide that option if the people aboard that plane wanted it badly enough. If they were willing to risk their own lives to keep memory alive than the forests around Katyn were willing to accept that sacrifice. The forests took those bodies in and made of them a new tragedy. The process of forgetting was reset back to zero. The past had become the present.

***

Except for one thing. History works even more strangely than that. The immediate result of the plane crash was to make the original loss, the original pain of Katyn fresh again. Amongst some Poles and some Russians, the language of friendship and reconciliation was replaced with the language of blame and mistrust. The theme of "moving on" reverted very quickly to the theme of "never forget." The old Katyn was stepping out of history to make its claims upon the new. People were beginning to freak out, to go back to the dark place of accusations and condemnation. The hard wing of Polish nationalism, led by Lech Kaczynski's twin brother, Jaroslaw Kaczynski, tried its best to inject an element of blame into the affair. The forces that want to remember Katyn at any cost realize, instinctively, that they need controversy, they need the possibility of guilt in order to keep this second Katyn connected meaningfully to the emotions of the first. There have been angry accusations about the events around the plane crash and what Russia could and should have done to prevent the tragedy. There has been controversy over the final report about the crash and whether it has been properly translated into English. There has been controversy over the burial of Lech Kaczynski, who was given (wrongly, some thought) a hero's burial in a tomb at Wawel Cathedral next to the great Polish Nationalist, defeater of the Soviet Red Army, and head of the Second Republic, Josef Pilsudski. All of this is the noise of the first Katyn rising up from the forest floor and doing its best to make its claims upon the second Katyn, to assert its memory in the present.

But the shock of the plane crash, its arbitrary nature, which was in such contrast to the intentional criminality of the first Katyn, had a completely different effect. People began to realize that there really is no one to blame for this second Katyn. The voices screaming 'never forget' are dashed against the pointless and accidental nature of the plane crash. This second Katyn is not like the first Katyn at all. This is what Timothy Garton Ash wrote in The Guardian just days after the plane crash: "The first Katyn catastrophe was concealed for decades by the night and fog of totalitarian lies; the second was immediately the lead item in news bulletins around the world. Most extraordinary has been the reaction of the former KGB officer Vladimir Putin, who has gone to exceptional lengths to demonstrate Russian sympathy, repeatedly visiting the crash site, announcing a national day of mourning today, and ordering Andrzej Wajda's film Katyn (which spares you nothing of the cruelty of the KGB's forerunners) to be shown on primetime Russian TV." Kris Kotarski, a journalist whose grandfather was a victim of the Katyn massacres, wrote that, "recent Russian gestures, both before and after the plane accident, mean so much to the people of Poland and offer so much hope for reconciliation."

The stupid pointlessness of the second Katyn has prevented it from having any real connection to the first. The supplement it provides is not one that awakens the pain and anger of the original massacre so much as a desire finally to go ahead and start forgetting. The second Katyn erases the painful memory of the first by being blameless, by coming into history for no reason and without inherent meaning. The first Katyn was an act of men, it was carried out by human beings for specific reasons. The second Katyn was an accident. And so, finally, in a twist if history no one would have expected, a memorial to a plane crash in the forests around Smolensk becomes the necessary tool for forgetting that the original memorial to the massacre of Katyn could not provide on its own. The people who wanted most to remember had to die so that the rest of us could begin to forget.

Section from "Relationship" series © Nikolay Bakharev

Ostalgia

Ostalgia is a dangerous art show. The name alone tells you that. It is troubling that a term like 'Ostalgia' exists at all. The term first gained popularity in Berlin after the Wall came down in 1989. By the mid-1990s, some people were feeling nostalgic for the divided Berlin that had so suddenly passed away. The term "*ostalgie*" was born. *Ost* is the German word for East, so *Ostalgie* was a coinage referring to that feeling of having lost a part of the city, the East part. That specific form of nostalgia made some sense in Berlin. Whatever the horrors and heartbreak of The Berlin Wall, it was a modern icon. The divided city of Berlin was like the official headquarters of the Cold War. When the Wall came down, there was general euphoria. The divisions of the past were being overcome. East Berlin was quickly pulled into the Western orbit. Berlin became whole again, but the price of wholeness was the loss of its importance as a Cold War capital. As the entire city was Westernized, it simultaneously became less unique.

Fast forwarding to the present, a sense of confusion and loss is still felt by many for the forgotten world that was the communist east. The *Ostalgia* show at The New Museum explores that feeling in the art of persons from the countries of the former Soviet Bloc; countries like East Germany, Yugoslavia, Romania, Hungary, Poland, and the Soviet Union itself. The press release for the show explains itself: "Zigzagging across distant geographies and personal histories, 'Ostalgia' composes an imaginary landscape, tracing the cartography of the dreams that haunted the East, for ultimately *'Ostalgia'* is an exhibition about myths and their demise." This is roughly as meaningless an explanation as it sounds. But we can be sympathetic to the nervous tone and imprecise language. That's because Ostalgia the art show, just like ostalgia the word, is about feelings of longing for a past we are supposed to despise. It is the longing that ought not be named.

There is a serious proposition here, a serious question. Was there something good about communism? Was there something decent about the form of life that existed behind the Iron Curtain? As a political question, this can be answered definitively in the negative. Soviet-style communism was a failure by definition. It couldn't sustain itself. It was also a system that relied—in its Stalinist period—on outright terror. Its totalitarian tendencies continued past the Stalinist days. Even in the relatively benign incarnation of the 70s and 80s, the world of the Soviet Empire was a world of political repression and the stifling of civil society. We are all aware of these facts. Indeed, they are so comfortable that we never seem to tire of repeating them. That is also why an art show like Ostalgia hides behind imprecise language and an ambivalence of purpose. It is a show that doesn't want to be caught taking the wrong political line. We are assured—in the explanations of artwork, in the press releases, in the catalogue, and in much of the work chosen—that this is a show that will do its job in critiquing the evils of communism.

But that is not what drove the curators at The New Museum to put up a show called Ostalgia. No one is interested in a show that condemns the politics of a civilization that no longer exists. In fact, the core impulse of Ostalgia is to explore a feeling that has nothing directly to do with politics at all. What art can show us about the society of the former Soviet Bloc is something that discussions of politics and society don't have immediate access to. Art can show us the immediacy of life as it was felt and experienced in that time, in that place.

What we find in Ostalgia is surprising. We find a great deal of ease. I'm not talking about material comfort or an "easy life." I am talking about human ease, to coin a term. Take a series of photographs (the "Relationship" series) by Nikolay Bakharev. One shot from the late 70s shows what seems to be a picnic in a park. Two young men are leaning against a tree. The one standing between two branches looks out at the camera, sort of, or just past it. The point is that he is both aware of the camera and indifferent to it. This is an attitude that would seem to be very difficult to fake, especially for someone who is not a professional model. So we can assume that his relative indifference is genuine. He wears a bathing suit but is not particularly concerned about his near-nakedness one way or the other. Looking at the picture, you want to say that he is just there. Even as he poses between the trunks of the tree he looks utterly at ease with whatever image of himself is going to be captured and preserved for posterity. He is presenting himself to the camera in a way that doesn't present anything, if that is possible. His gestures and his facial features confront that camera in the same way that they might confront a friend, or nothing at all. He would be there between the trees even if a camera were nowhere to be found, even if he were alone and simply being in nature. I don't want to say that he is showing us his "true self". Maybe we can say that he is showing us his "self unencumbered." The second young man holds his left arm behind his back grasping the tree branch on the right side. It is a gesture so utterly innocent, so simultaneously exposed and self-confident that it is difficult to give it a name. We don't encounter that kind of un-posed posing in daily life very much anymore.

This is not to say that people in the former Soviet Bloc were without worries or unconcerned about how they presented themselves to others. Communist life demanded that citizens take up a public persona of good-citizenship that was often so absurd and contrary to the actual facts of daily life that it required willful schizophrenia just to pull it off. There was a lot of pretending in life behind the Iron Curtain. But there was a realm of privacy in the former Soviet Bloc in which people seem to have been able to escape that social pressure and be free from the need to act out any role at all. In the private sphere, the pressure of being this or that was suddenly released. Maybe the freedom came partly from the fact that the private sphere did not, officially, exist. And that is when what I am calling 'human ease' emerges. It emerges when 'just being' can take precedence over 'being x' or 'being y'. That guy standing between the trees in the Bakharev photo is not 'a plumber' or 'a party official' or 'an aspiring actor' or 'a disappointed guy who had a lot of potential'. If anything, the photograph makes me want to describe him as "a human being, being human."

Many of Bakharev's photos from the 70s and 80s have this quality. The same thing can be found in the film clips put together by Neil Cummings and Marysia Lewandowska, (Enthusiasm. The Films of Love, Longing, and Labour, 2004). Cummings and Lewandowska rescued and restored a number of amateur film clips from communist Poland. In them can be found the same postures and attitudes of human ease that are so striking in the photographs of Bakharev. Being films, we get to see people moving. It is possible, watching these clips, to say that people moved differently in the Eastern Bloc and especially in their moments of privacy. Is it possible to say that the movement is both awkward and fluid at the same time? Like the un-posed posing of Bakharev's photographs, the movement is distinguished by a lack of prepossession. Rarely do the people in these films seem as if they are watching themselves move, or second-guessing how their acts of movement might look on film, even though they are often aware of being filmed.

The same phenomenon is revealed in the snapshots by Boris Mikhailov. Mikhailov has a taste for perversion and deviant behavior that gives his photographs a special quality. But even in his snapshots of people being naughty from the 60s and 70s there is the same projection of human ease. Taking nude pictures was, technically, illegal during the days of the Soviet Union. But many of the nude subjects Mikhailov captures project no defiance whatsoever. Something different is going on. They are expressing their freedom not by challenging the politics of the day but by challenging the idea that they need to be political at all. They are under no constraint. And being under no constraint, they have little if anything to prove, to themselves or to anyone else. They confront Mikhailov's camera as guileless and unassuming as children. Indeed, there is a childlike quality to all of these photographs. Maybe it comes from the fact that children don't yet know exactly who they are when they stand in front of the camera. Mikhailov's subjects are like that, they do not know who to be. Unlike children, however, they seem to recognize this as an achievement. They accept that relative simplicity of being. They are proud of it. They have joy.

In a contemporary culture in which we are constantly told about the virtue of creating our own identities, of making ourselves whoever we want to be, it is striking to see the self-presentation of human beings living in a society that did not recognize that same virtue. The idea that each human being is in charge of his or her own identity, his or her own "brand", did not exist behind the Iron Curtain. You had to play your public role, you had to utter the public lies, and then the rest of the time the stakes dropped way down. There wasn't much further pressure to be this or that. Individual ambition had few avenues for expression anyway. Working on your personal brand would have been a waste of time. In fact, it would more than likely have been counter-productive, making one into a suspicious character.

So, we must confront another difficult idea. It was, in fact, the political repression that made the moments of 'human ease' in the private sphere possible. The stultifying pointlessness of public life in the Soviet Bloc, its stupidity and its demand for constant lies was the cost. That was the price every citizen had to pay. Because everything was at stake in one's public role as citizen, there was almost nothing at stake in being a human the rest of the time. Do, therefore, the souls of actual human beings qua their humanness stare out of the films and photographs of that period? Because these people don't have anything to gain, they don't try to gain much. Because they don't have any reason to protect themselves from the camera or from the potential viewer, they project something internal, something that seems very, very real.

This is what we see in the lost world of the Soviet era. It is impossible to want it because wanting it means wanting a whole structure of repression and totalitarianism in order to get it. It would be crazy to choose a bad politics in the hope that one might get a few moments of human ease in the backyard now and again.

But art is indifferent to our desires and indifferent to the problems of politics and society. Art simply shows us what is there. The artists of the Soviet Bloc could not help but capture the special private world that existed in the decades of the waning of that empire. The photographer or filmmaker was able, in those private moments, to fade out of existence and to capture human beings presenting themselves to the camera as if it were of no consequence. Try to do that now. It is extremely difficult. Even without the knowledge that your photograph will probably be uploaded to Facebook it is extremely difficult to pose for a picture without thinking about how you want to be and who you want to be seen as. And that is what we long for, despite ourselves, when we look back to that time. We want the human ease just to be. We see something essentially human gazing out at us from a lost world. We can't be that way, we don't know how to be that way; it is impossible, maybe, to be that way. But we want it.

The Mezzanine

The great 20th century novelist William Gaddis once wrote, "That's what my work is about, the collapse of everything, of meaning, of language, of values, of art, disorder and dislocation wherever you look, entropy drowning everything in sight." Gaddis was born in 1922. He was an unabashed theorist of decline. For him, the novelist's task was to narrate that decline, all the way until there was nothing left to say, until language itself gave up the ghost and we'd be left with a literature of empty mumbling.

Alas, just when things seemed like they might truly fall apart for Gaddis' generation, the next comes along and makes sense of the chaos. Human beings are known to adapt. Give each historical catastrophe long enough to settle and the world simply becomes the world again. Thus has the dilemma always been for the apocalyptic mind. It is a mind well suited to show us how bad things really are, but ill-suited to recognize the staying power of that essential badness.

In a funny way, I see Nicholson Baker's *The Mezzanine* as a sequel to the work of William Gaddis. I say that because they describe the same world. It is a world of meaningless work and a language hopelessly diluted into the jargon of commercial transactions and the exchange of goods and services. Baker's world is as empty as Gaddis ever said it would be. And yet, it is not.

Baker's protagonist is a man who spends the entirety of the short novel traveling up an escalator to the mezzanine of the corporate building where his office can be found. His job, a nameless one. His relationships, superficial and generally characterized by office chit-chat. The novel spends most of its time following the narrator's train of thought as his attention wanders from one mundane subject to the next. But Baker manages to show that within this "empty" experience is, in fact, a richness of human subjectivity vast and complicated as to be a wonder.

On page 72 of the Vintage edition of the book, published in 1988, Baker comes as close as he ever does to stating his purpose. Baker's narrator is musing upon the achievements of mechanical engineering that can be found in the corporate bathroom:

> Valves that allow a controlled amount of water to rush into a toilet and no more, shapes of porcelain designed so that the turbulence in them forms almost fixed and decorative (yet highly functional) braids and twists that Hopkins would have liked; a little built-in machine that squirts pink liquefied soap with a special additive that gives it a silvery sheen (also used in shampoo recipes now, I've noticed) into the curve of your fingers; and the soap-level indicator, a plastic fish-eye directly into the soap tank, that shows the maintenance man (either Ray or the very one who was now polishing the escalator's handrail) whether he must unlock the brushed-steel panel that day and replenish the supply; the beautiful chrome-plated urinal plumbing, a row of four identical states of severe gnarledness, which gives you the impression of walking into a petrochemical plant, with

names like Sloan Valve and Delaney Flushboy inscribed on their six-sided half-decorative boltlike caps—names that become completely familiar over the course of your employment even though if asked you couldn't come up with them.

It's the reference to Gerard Manley Hopkins that interests me most here. "Look at the world we are given just as Hopkins looked at his," Baker seems to be saying. And then he goes out and does just that. Hopkins called this way of looking "inscape." He said, "Poetry is in fact speech employed to carry the inscape of speech for the inscape's sake." What he meant was simply that poetry had to pay very close attention to the specific complexity that makes each thing unique. Inscape is that inner uniqueness. Baker, contra Gaddis and in a Hopkins frame of mind, suggests that we are not any more or less able to reflect on experience and "inscape" now than at any other time. All that's required is a touch of enthusiasm. I mean that in the ancient sense of the term, the Greek sense of the term. For the Greeks, enthusiasm was about *entheos* or being possessed by a God. It was sort of like channeling. It meant that one had become a vehicle to express something beyond oneself. To be entheos is thus to be fully absorbed. This is almost the exact opposite of the stance Gaddis takes toward the world and his prose. Gaddis wants to reproduce the language of his time in order to make the reader aware of its degradation. He wants to be in language just long enough to get outside it and see it as a whole. That's how he can express the world and condemn it at the same time.

Baker's enthusiasm goes head over heels in its immersion. It thus has little to say about the world as such, the era, the relative progress or decline of history. Baker's narrator simply lets himself go, lets himself interrogate every detail and think through every interaction ad nauseam. The result is an estrangement of the world that, paradoxically, brings it ever closer. The more intently one thinks about what it is really like to tie your shoes, the more it seems a wondrous and fantastical activity and the more, then, we are able to see ourselves as that weird combination of happenstance and habit that is so very human. This is what Hopkins wanted to accomplish in his poetry, to concentrate so intently on the details that the divinity would arise therein. Baker operates without the implicit theology. But he does think that the details will illuminate us, capture us, as it were, in the activities that mark us as a specific people at a specific time. The world, our world. If nothing else, it is inexhaustible in its fascination.

Morgan Meis

CPSIA information can be obtained
at www.ICGtesting.com
Printed in the USA
LVOW04s1207250716
497671LV00003B/254/P